Praise for the original French edition

"An intellectually original and
undeniably pugnacious endeavor."
—PATRICK PIRO, *Politis*

"[A] bombshell book."
—LOUIS-GILLES FRANCOEUR, *Le Devoir*

"An invigorating book, to be read at once."
—*L'Ecologiste*

"A vigorous indictment against the 'neoliberal ideology,'
guilty of driving the planet towards its own destruction."
—OLIVIER NOUAILLAS, *La Vie*

"Stunning survey . . . great journalism."
—ANNE CRIGNON, *Le Nouvel Observateur*

HOW
THE
RICH
ARE
DESTROYING
THE
EARTH

HERVÉ KEMPF

HOW THE RICH ARE

DESTROYING

THE EARTH

HERVÉ KEMPF

FOREWORD BY GREG PALAST

Translated from the
French by Leslie Thatcher

green books

This edition first published in the UK in 2008
by Green Books
Foxhole, Dartington, Totnes, Devon TQ9 6EB
www.greenbooks.co.uk

Originally published in France as *Comment les riches détruisent la planète*
by Editions du Seuil in 2007.

This UK edition is based on the English-language edition published
in the USA & Canada by Chelsea Green, White River Junction, Vermont, USA.

Book Designer: Peter Holm, Sterling Hill Productions
Cover designer: David Drummond

Text printed on 100% recycled paper (100% post-consumer waste).
Covers printed on 80% recycled material.

Printed in the UK by TJ International, Padstow, Cornwall.

British Library Cataloguing in Publication data available on request.

ISBN 978 1 900322 41 6

CONTENTS

FOREWORD

So why the hell shouldn't the rich destroy the planet? After all, it's theirs. They own it. We all live on it, true, but we're just renting space from the Landlords of our piece of earth, our air, our water.

The Landlords do what they want with their property. To get at their gold, they dump arsenic in our drinking water; to get at their oil, they melt our polar caps and pump soot into our lungs.

Hervé Kempf, being French, is really upset about this. But many Westerners applaud it. We call these resource rapists "entrepreneurs"—it's the only French word most journalists know—and drool over their rewards in *Hello* and *OK! Magazine*.

It's a weirdly perfect day to be writing an introduction to Kempf's *J'accuse*. The United States Supreme Court has just let Exxon off the hook for spewing oil all over the Alaskan coastline with the crude that poured from the tanker Exxon Valdez. Years back, I investigated that eco-horror for the people that lived on the slimed beaches, the indigenous Chugach of Alaska.

What I found was that the oil would have never touched the coast if the company had surrounded the ship with a rubber barrier immediately after it ran aground. That's exactly the kind of barrier the oil shipper swore, before the spill, that it would have at the ready—right on the island where the ship hit. But they didn't. Exxon lied—under oath—then lied again in writing, and then lied again to cover up the fact that they'd placed no oil spill equipment on the island. Ten months before the spill, at a secret meeting of the executives of the world's largest oil companies, Exxon's top brass vetoed a plea from their own vice president in Alaska to buy the oil spill containment equipment. Exxon didn't want to spend the money.

The savings to Exxon in safety equipment not purchased ran into the billions. The damage to our planet was inestimable. The damage to the Alaskan people can be measured in bankruptcies and suicides.

And that's what Kempf is telling us: Ecological destruction is a profitable business.

He busts the myth that somehow there is no connection between the black oil in the water and the black ink on the bottom line.

We continue to pretend that destroying our planet is somehow the result of working-class vices, like driving to work or not recycling our juice bottles. Saving the planet, we are told, is the work of our enlightened rulers. After all, British Petroleum has painted all its petrol stations green.

Kempf dissents. He explains that you can't have a grossly consuming over-class without driving the underclass to desperation. Raise the price of oil to over $100 a barrel, and the poor of Indonesia will cut down forests for fuel to cook their food.

Kempf gets it: Environmental devastation is class war by other means. It's not about attitudes or habits, not about tree huggers versus tree cutters. Not about Labour versus Conservatives or Democrats versus Republicans. It's the rich versus the rest of us. Barrick Gold Corporation, once infused by cash from Saudi gun-runner Adnan Khashoggi and named an "Environmental Pig of the Year" by one U.S. magazine, has had on its payroll George Bush Sr., one-time civil rights leader Andrew Young, Vernon Jordan (Bill Clinton's lawyer), right-wing Latin media mogul Gustavo Cisneros, former Canadian Prime Minister Brian Mulroney, former U.S. Defense Secretary William Cohen, and banker Nathaniel Rothschild. That just tells you that these little piggies come in Black and White, Democrat and Republican, Tory and Liberal, speaking French and English and Hindi, too. They are Protestant, Jewish, Catholic, Muslim, and Satanic. A rainbow coalition of hyper-rich worldwide destructo-crats holding hands across the continents.

No one understands this better than the inventor of the modern environmental movement, Barry Commoner. The accomplished biologist, now 91 years old, working in the 1950s with soulful, large minds like Linus Pauling, conceived of a movement that would marry biological science, earth sciences, conservationism, the Ban-the-Bomb movement—and class war. Commoner was, after World War II, a secret member of the Communist Party, a connection he now regrets, given the murderous treatment of the planet by the Soviets. Nevertheless, his Marx-informed understanding of the politics of eco-imperialism taught him that saving the planet—and the creatures on it—requires knowing your enemy, those who assault Mother Earth to make a buck.

Kempf, knowingly or unknowingly, is Commoner's child. Kempf understands, it's us versus them. I, by contrast, am the bastard offspring of Commoner's nemesis, Milton Friedman, under whom I studied at the University of Chicago. The Milton Friedman school of economics calls crimes against our planet "externalities" which must steadfastly be ignored in the drive for wealth creation. It's a damaged theory of markets uber alles in which Democrats and Republicans alike would have us trade in our factory jobs so that the real bosses can have bigger yachts and summer homes.

As Kempf notes, it was also at the University of Chicago where, in 1892, the theory of the "leisure class" as economic leeches was first studied by professor Thorsten Veblen. "Conspicuous consumption" was Veblen's term, and it remains today's leisure class game. Kempf, imploring us to raise Veblen from the dead, does so with the urgency of a most clever environmentalist and the frustration of a fed-up socialist. He argues for more equitable control of this planet as the only answer to the earth's degradation.

Kempf gets it: The rising sea level is a direct consequence of rising inequality. Yet the knights of the new world order, like George Bush, Al Gore, or the CEO of a multi-national that is telling you to reduce your carbon footprint from their private jet, want you to believe the solution lies with turning our fate over to enlightened business chieftains. It was, let's remember, that supreme hot-air salesman, Mr. Gore, who sold us the fable of "free trade," forcing the North America Free Trade Agreement (NAFTA) down our throats. Thanks to Al's NAFTA, we're all sucking diesel soot from tractor trailers hauling cheap goods to Wal-Mart, where now laid-off workers from shut-down U.S. factories shop for bargains. It was Gore who ran a crusade against environmental and safety regulations in the Clinton Administration, all in the name of "efficient" (translation: corporate-friendly) government. Dubya Bush only took Al's get-out-of-the-way-of-markets philosophy to its nasty conclusion.

When the anti-regulation, free-market psychosis leads to illness in our environment, the two connected forces—grotesque market profiteering and planetary corrosion—are made to seem innocuously distinct. Kempf shows us that they are just two arms of the same beast. He suggests we wise up, and quick. The ultimate obstacle to Earth's salvation is our own naiveté.

GREG PALAST
June 26, 2008

PREFACE

I had just finished writing a story about the "soldier of the future," and I was on the bus to Heathrow Airport when I heard the news on the radio. The reporter explained that, according to Swedish experts, a high level of radioactivity that could have arisen from a nuclear-power station accident had been detected in that Scandinavian country.

It was April 28, 1986, the day after the Chernobyl accident. For me, that news suddenly reawakened a feeling of forgotten urgency. Ten or fifteen years before, I had read Ivan Illich, *La Gueule ouverte* ("Open Mouth," the first environmental magazine, founded in 1972), and *Le Sauvage* (another ecology magazine, associated with *Le Nouvel Observateur*, that came out in 1973) and had been enthralled by ecology, which seemed to be the only real alternative at a time when Marxism was triumphant.

Then life pushed me in other directions. As a journalist, I was immersed in the microcomputing revolution. At a time when *Time* magazine crowned the computer "Man of the Year", I, along with my colleagues from *Science et Vie Micro*, was discovering the arcana of the first Macintosh, Minitel's *messageries roses* (literally, "pink messages", an online service of France Telecom) that prefigured adult Internet forums and chat rooms, and the adventures of a young guy named Bill Gates who had just concluded a smoking deal with IBM.

Then suddenly – Chernobyl. There was an overwhelmingly obvious need: to think about ecology. And there was an exigency: to report about it. I began to do just that. Since then, I have always been guided by two rules: to be independent, and to produce good information that is precise, pertinent, and original. Also, I held back from doomsdayism. While I was among the first to write about climate issues, the genetically modified organism (GMO) adventure and the biodiversity crisis, I have never exaggerated. It seems to me that the facts, presented with tenacious attention to such obviously important subjects, are sufficient to speak to our intellect. And I believed that intelligence would be sufficient to transform the world.

However, after having believed that things would change, that society would evolve and that the system could improve, today I make two observations: first, the planet's ecological situation is worsening at a speed that the efforts of millions—but too few—of the world's citizens who are aware of the drama have not succeeded in slowing down. Second, the social system that presently governs human society—capitalism—blindly sticks to its guns and resists the changes that are indispensable if we want to preserve the dignity and promise of human existence.

These two observations led me to throw my weight—however minimal it may be—onto the scales by writing this book, which is short and as clear as possible without oversimplifying. I am sounding an alarm here, but above all, making a double appeal upon which the future success of everything depends: to ecologists, to think about social arrangements and power relationships; to those who think about social arrangements, to take the true measure of the ecological crisis and how it relates to justice.

The comfort in which Western societies are immersed must not conceal us from the gravity of the moment. We are entering a time of lasting crisis and possible catastrophe. Signs of the ecological crisis are clearly visible, and the hypothesis of a catastrophe is becoming realistic.

Yet, in reality, people pay little attention to these signs. They influence neither politics nor the economy. The system does not know how to change trajectory. Why?

Because we are not able to see the interrelationship of ecology and society.

However, we cannot understand the concomitance of the ecological and social crises if we don't analyze them as the two sides of the same disaster. And that disaster derives from a system piloted by a dominant social stratum that today has no drive other than greed, no ideal other than conservatism, and no dream other than technology.

This predatory oligarchy is the main agent of the global crisis—directly, by the decisions it makes. Those decisions aim to maintain the order that has been established to favour the objective of material growth, which is the only method, according to the oligarchy, to make the subordinate classes accept the injustice of the social situation.

But material growth intensifies environmental degradation.

The oligarchy also exercises a powerful indirect influence as a result of the cultural attraction its consumption habits exercise on society as a whole, and especially on the middle class. In the best-provided-for countries, as in developing countries, a large share of consumption satisfies a desire for ostentation and distinction. People aspire to lift themselves up the social ladder, which happens through imitation of the superior class's consumption habits. Thus, the oligarchy diffuses its ideology of waste throughout the whole society.

The oligarchy's behaviour not only leads to the deepening of the crises. Faced with opposition to its privileges, with environmental anxiety, with criticism of economic neoliberalism, it also weakens public freedoms and the spirit of democracy.

A drift toward semi-authoritarian regimes may be observed almost everywhere in the world. The oligarchy that reigns in the

United States is its engine, using the fear that the terrorist attacks of 11th September 2001 elicited in U.S. society.

In this situation, which could lead to either social chaos or dictatorship, it is important to know what is right for us and for future generations to maintain: not 'the Earth', but "the possibilities of human life on the planet," as philosopher Hans Jonas calls them; that is, humanism, the values of mutual respect and tolerance, a restrained and rich relationship with nature, and cooperation among human beings.

To achieve those goals, it is not enough for society to become aware of the urgency of the ecological crisis—and of the difficult choices that preventing the crisis imposes, notably in terms of material consumption. What is necessary is that ecological concerns be articulated in a radical political analysis of current relationships of domination. We will not be able to decrease global material consumption if the powerful are not brought down and if inequality is not combated. To the ecological principle that was so useful at the time we first became aware— 'Think globally; act locally'—we must add the principle that the present situation imposes: 'Consume less; share better.'

1 | CATASTROPHE. AND THEN WHAT?

The night had been long. Exhausting, but thrilling. In a final twist, Russia had posed a major obstacle to the compromise that had come out of a week of bitter negotiations. Was the Kyoto Protocol going to fail after having triumphed over American obstinacy? However, over the course of the nocturnal consultations skillfully conducted by Canadian and English diplomats, Russia withdrew its—incidentally, incomprehensible—demand, and the agreement was cemented: the global community decided to extend the protocol beyond its expiry date of 2012, and the new giants, China and India, acceded in coded terms to this dialogue that would inevitably engage them in the challenges of the future.

These international negotiations resembled a cosmopolitan caravan composed of shimmering faces and diverse interests, passions, and egotisms, but animated also, behind the clash of interests, by a common belief in the necessity of a universal agreement. Behind the obscure rituals and esoteric texts, the ideal of a policy for all humanity was being implemented. And everyone there in that room in Montreal in December 2005—men and women, their features drawn, eyes swollen, extremities numb—applauded and laughed at the good news.

Having forgotten that the night could be a sleepless one, I had scheduled a meeting the following morning with an eminent scientist to talk about a completely different subject: biodiversity. As I walked in the cold air of the Québec metropolis, carried along by the enthusiasm of the preceding hours, I was unconscious of my fatigue and was feeling, I admit, rather perky.

Through the window of Michel Loreau's narrow office, we could see the tall buildings of the city, a totally artificial universe. And in his precise language, without an ounce of exaggeration or emotion, with the calm appropriate to the director of the international research program Diversitas, the Belgian researcher told me what I already knew, but which, in the crystalline light of a Canadian winter, took on a dramatic significance I had not perceived in full measure until then. The planet Earth is experiencing at this very moment the sixth extinction crisis of living species that it has known since life began to transform its mineral surface some three billion years ago. "Today," he told me, "we deem that the rate of extinction among the best-known groups—vertebrates and plants—is a hundred times higher than it was on average in geological eras, apart from crises of mass extinction." He paused. "That's already a lot, but it's nothing compared to what is forecast: that rate is going to accelerate and be of the order of ten thousand times higher than the geological rate."

James Lovelock is almost unknown in France. That fact is testament to the environmental illiteracy that reigns in my country, because in Great Britain, but also in Japan, Germany, Spain, and the United States, the great savant enjoys a deserved fame. That's because he has advanced science on two fronts: on the one hand, by inventing a series of apparatuses very useful to physicists—in particular, the electron capture detector—and on the other hand, by elaborating a theory of our planet that numbers among the most intellectually stimulating that exist. He has named this theory Gaia, at the suggestion of his friend, the Nobel laureate in literature William Golding. According to Lovelock, the Earth behaves like a self-regulating living organism.

But if I snaked along the little roads of Cornwall, crossing a countryside that has somehow managed to keep its nineteenth-century rural character, it was not to talk about Gaia but to hear the great savant's pessimistic message. There were two reasons to pay attention to my host's argument: his impressive curriculum vitae, and his comprehensive knowledge, received straight from the best sources, of the climate debates. In fact, he frequently talks with climatologists from the Hadley Research Centre in Exeter, fifty kilometres from his home. Hadley is one of the most highly respected centres in the world on the subject of climate matters. Later, in discussions with other researchers and through reading, I would confirm the worrying message that Lovelock delivered to me.

"With global warming," he said to me in the very British atmosphere of his little white house, "most of the surface of the globe will change into desert. The survivors will gather around the Arctic. But there won't be enough room for everybody, so there will be wars, raging populations, warlords. It's not the Earth that is threatened, but civilization."

"I am a happy man; I don't like catastrophe tales," he continued. "That's what makes this one so strange—before, I didn't think the danger was so big."

May Professor Lovelock forgive me, but I could have uttered that last sentence word for word on my own account. I have been following the question of climate change closely since 1988. I have observed how concern has developed among scientists, emerged in the media, and then confronted contradictory arguments before solidifying into a framework for a firmly based interpretation of the world. The dawning of awareness progressed with virtually stupefying speed, and many researchers are more pessimistic than they ever imagined they could be fifteen years ago. There's no 'catastrophism' here, or else one must consider the whole scientific community catastrophist.

For some time now, a problematic piece of news has been worrying climatologists, and that is that the climate could be brutally disturbed at a rate too fast for human action to correct the disequilibrium. That's the worry that Lovelock expresses—freer in his speech than other scientists, but still without exaggerating their concern.

Goal: Limiting the Damage

A scientific theory elaborated upon as early as the nineteenth century, the idea of global warming was rediscovered during the 1970s and studied attentively from 1980 onwards. An intense discussion among scientists followed.

Climate change is due to the growth in the greenhouse effect: certain gases, such as carbon dioxide and methane, have the property of trapping part of the heat the Earth reflects back into space. Because of the recent accumulation of these gases in the atmosphere, the planet's average temperature is increasing.

The idea that climate change has already begun rests on three advances in observation: the level of carbon dioxide and other gases in the atmosphere continues to mount; the average temperature of the globe regularly increases; and the quality of the physical models of the biosphere and of other instruments to understand climate has improved significantly.

According to the Intergovernmental Panel on Climate Change (IPCC), which brings together the community of scientists specializing in climate change, the increase in average temperature at the end of the twenty-first century, based on a projection of present tendencies, should be between 1.4 and 5.8 degrees Celsius*. And it wouldn't stop there. If nothing changes between now and the end of the century, this warming will continue.

These apparently modest numbers are in fact significant. The

---

*A change of 1 degree Celsius is equivalent to a change of 1.8 degrees Fahrenheit.

globe's average temperature is 15 degrees Celsius. A few degrees are enough to provoke a radical change in the climatic regime. For example, less than 3 degrees Celsius separates us from the Holocene, from 6,000 to 8,000 years ago; similarly, the average temperature during the Ice Age 20,000 years ago was only 5 degrees Celsius less than that of today.

Even if we were suddenly to stop our gas emissions all at once, the increase in the greenhouse effect provoked by the previous emissions would not be immediately halted. In fact, many greenhouse gases have a chemical stability of several decades, which means their properties persist in the atmosphere for a long time. Natural systems possess significant amounts of inertia: slow to change, they are equally slow to regain their previous state. We can no longer hope to return rapidly to the situation that existed before the middle of the nineteenth century—the time when, in the course of the industrial revolution, the massive emissions of greenhouse gases began. On the other hand, we can slow down the acceleration of those emissions, aiming at their stabilization, then their reduction. That would allow us to limit warming to 2 to 3 degrees Celsius. In reality, that has become the only realistic objective.

If the Climate Were to Spiral Out of Control . . .

A crucial element for understanding the present situation relates to the time scale: the warming that we are living through is happening very rapidly compared to comparable phenomena experienced in the past, that took place over thousands of years; we are transforming the climate system in less than two hundred years.

And climate change, instead of occurring gradually, could strike suddenly. In a few decades, the climate could swing several degrees, preventing society from adapting in a gradual way. That discovery, made in the beginning of the 1990s, is expressed today in another way: beyond a certain threshold—which climatologists place at around 2 degrees Celsius of warming—the climate system could spiral irreversibly out of control. Normally, the biosphere spontaneously corrects disturbances that affect it. But because of the saturation of its absorption capacities, this restorative process could no longer take place. Here are the mechanisms that could lead to climate change spiraling out of control:

- A big share of the carbon gases humanity emits is ordinarily sucked up by vegetation and the oceans: half remains in the atmosphere, and a quarter is absorbed by the oceans and a quarter by vegetation. That's why the oceans and continental vegetation are called carbon gas 'sinks'. Now, if these sinks become saturated, a greater proportion of the emitted carbon gas, even its entirety, would remain in the atmosphere, accelerating the greenhouse effect still further. The oceans and vegetation could even begin to release the CO_2 they had previously stored. On top of that, continued deforestation could transform tropical forests, which are still carbon sinks, into net carbon emitters.
- The Arctic and Antarctic regions are warming. Several series of observations and calculations lead glaciologists to think that Greenland and the Antarctic continent could melt rapidly, which would entail a greater rise in sea level than the IPCC envisioned in 2001. It forecast a half metre of rise by the end of the century; revised calculations would have to begin with a rise of two or three metres, or even more.

- The polar ice—like any white surface—reflects sunlight, thus limiting the warming of the Earth's surface. This is known as the 'albedo effect'. But the progressive melting of the polar ice reduces the albedo effect and its limitation of warming, consequently stimulating warming.
- In the same way, the warming of the high latitudes— more accentuated, apparently, than that of the rest of the planet—would entail the thaw of the permafrost, a layer of frozen earth that covers over a million square kilometres, mostly in Siberia, to a depth of twenty-five metres on average. It is estimated that the permafrost stores five hundred billion tons of carbon that would be released if it melted.

These phenomena remain hypothetical. But several studies suggest that they could come true. For example, a group of researchers showed that during the summer heat wave of 2003, Europe's vegetation, instead of absorbing carbon gases, released a significant quantity of them. Other researchers have shown that the permafrost is beginning to thaw; if that continues "at the rate observed," the authors write, "all the carbon recently stored could be released during the century." Moreover, recent analyses maintain that climate models have underestimated the interactions between greenhouse gases and the biosphere, which leads to the conclusion that warming will be more significant than the IPCC predicted in its 2007 report. These factors account for the scientific community's incorporating the possibility of a very rapid increase in the globe's average temperature to unbearable levels.

"Eight degrees of warming in a century is very unlikely, but it's no longer a low probability in two centuries if we use all the oil, develop oil shale, and burn half the coal," worries Stanford University's Stephen Schneider. In fact, the IPCC, in its fourth report published in 2007, considers that warming could exceed the maximum 5.8 degrees Celsius level that it had previously foreseen.

Not Seen Since the Dinosaurs

Although very much less known about than climate change, the global biodiversity crisis is no less worrying. Its most obvious indicator is the disappearance of living species, the rhythm of which is so rapid that the expression 'sixth extinction', following on the five previous major species-extinction crises the planet underwent even before the appearance of man, has become official: "We are, at present, responsible for the sixth major extinction in the history of the Earth and the most significant one since the dinosaurs disappeared 65 million years ago," asserts the *Report on Global Biodiversity* given during the United Nations Conference on biodiversity in Brazil in 2006.

Every year, the World Conservation Union publishes its threatened species 'red list'; in 2006, of the 40,177 species studied, 16,119 were threatened with extinction. "A substantial decline in the abundance and the diversity of fauna will occur over 50 to 90 percent of the Earth's surface by 2050, if the growth in infrastructure and the exploitation of terrestrial resources continues at its present pace," warns the Globio research centre from the United Nations Program for the Environment. Here again, the speed of the transformation of the Earth's environment by humanity, compared with the changes it has previously experienced, is mind-boggling; the experts, like Michel Loreau, agree that the rate of extinction of species are likely to reach thousands of times the natural rate found in geological history, that is, in the study of fossils.

The major cause of species disappearance is wear and tear on, or destruction of, habitats, which has reached a frenetic pace over the last half century: more land has been converted to agriculture since 1950 than during the entire eighteenth and nineteenth centuries, according to the Millennium Ecosystem Assessment, a report developed by over 1,300 scientists from around the world. Since 1980, 35 percent of mangroves (wet forests along tropical coasts) have been lost, as well as 20 percent of coral reefs; humanity's production of nitrogen exceeds that of all natural processes, while the quantity of water retained behind the great dams exceeds by three to six times that which flows through rivers and streams. "We have experienced more rapid change in the last thirty years than during any period in human history," summarizes Neville Ash from the World Conservation Monitoring Centre (UNEP-WCMC) in Cambridge, England. According to the Globio researchers, a third of the Earth's land surface has been converted to agriculture, and more than another third is in the process of transformation into agricultural, urban, or infrastructure use.

This transformation is not only the result of developing countries trying to cope with their immense needs. Rich countries are also wasting massive amounts of space. In France, the group Demonstrate for Landscapes, launched in 2005, observes that "urban sprawl is most often accompanied by an inordinate consumption of land capital, even though land capital constitutes a non-renewable resource: urban acreage has doubled since 1945, [and] artificial surfaces have increased 17 percent [over] the last ten years, while the population has only grown 4 percent."

All life forms are affected by this crisis in biodiversity. Virtually all the planet's natural habitats are now in an altered state. In fact, the Millennium Ecosystem Assessment's scientists warn that "human activity is exerting so much pressure on the planet's natural functions that ecosystems' capacity to respond to the demands of future generations can no longer be considered guaranteed."

The consequences of the loss of biodiversity are difficult to evaluate. Naturalists expect threshold effects—that is, brutal reactions from the ecosystems once certain imbalances have been reached: "One may compare biodiversity to a game of Mikado [pick-up sticks], and the loss of the sticks one withdraws one by one," says Jacques Weber, director of the French Institute of Biodiversity. "Take away one, then two: nothing moves. But one day, the pile could collapse in on itself." The Millennium Ecosystem Assessment expresses the same idea in another way: "The living machinery of the Earth has a tendency to go from gradual change to catastrophic change with hardly any warning. . . . Once such a breaking point has been reached, it may be difficult, even impossible for natural systems to revert to their previous state." In fact, as in the case of climate change, scientists are beginning to fear that we may cross a threshold beyond which brutal and irreversibly damaging phenomena will be set in motion.

We Are All Salmon

Besides the transformation of habitats—either by creating artificial ones, or by destroying them—there is generalized pollution that all indicators show to be growing. The world's biggest ecosystem—its oceans—is now appreciably deteriorating. "It is the victim of an unprecedented decline," summarizes Jean-Pierre Féral of the French National Centre for Scientific Research (CNRS). The marine mass, which covers 71 percent of the Earth's surface and which had been considered a boundless resource up until now, is beginning to show the limits of its ability to digest the rubbish created by human activity. The peaking and subsequent reduction in fishing catches are the most visible symptoms of this impoverishment of the seas: overexploited fish represented 10 percent of total fishing stocks during the 1970s, 24 percent in 2002, and have risen to a current 52 percent. While up until now the deterioration mainly affected coastal waters, it is now reaching the oceans' entirety: it is estimated, for example, that an average of 18,000 scraps of plastic float on every square kilometer of ocean; in the centre of the Pacific, there are three kilograms of garbage for every half kilogram of plankton. The high seas and the ocean depths, which shelter an extremely significant biodiversity, are beginning to be exploited and disturbed by fishing, prospecting for new species, oil research, et cetera.

One of the most distressing and symbolic signs of what we have done to the planet is taking place between the ocean and the lakes of Alaska. At the end of their lives, wild salmon return to spawn in the hundreds of lakes that state contains. They lay their eggs and then die, their bodies settling at the bottom of the lake to which their instinct led them. Canadian researchers decided to collect and analyze the sediments in one of these lakes, sediments composed in large part from the cadavers of the great migrating fish. They were surprised to discover that those sediments contained more polychlorinated biphenyls (PCBs) than could have been there from the action of atmospheric deposits alone. PCBs are highly persistent chemical pollutants that were used in huge quantities for decades during the twentieth century. These excess PCBs in the lakes come from the fish carcasses. So wild salmon pollute the immaculate lakes of the most remote regions of Alaska.

How has that happened? PCBs are spread throughout the ocean in minute amounts. During their peregrinations in the

North Pacific, the fish accumulate these polychlorinated biphenyls in their fatty tissue: while one finds less than a nanogram per litre in the ocean, the concentration in the fish's fatty tissue reaches 2,500 nanograms per gram of fat. The salmon 'act like biological pumps', accumulating toxins before returning to pollute the lake . . . and their progeny.

We are all salmon. As beings at the top of the food chain, our organisms accumulate contaminants broadly disseminated through the biosphere by our so-indispensable 'human activities.' And just as the Alaskan salmon poison their own progeny, so too do we contaminate our children from birth. In Germany, several public agencies have regularly analyzed mothers' milk for years, and they have observed that it contains up to 350 kinds of pollutants. These poisons are found not only in mother's milk. In the same way, all analyses of blood serum done in developed countries show that adults are contaminated—in small doses, to be sure—by a large range of chemical products.

Although it has not been clearly established to what degree generalized chemical contamination affects people's health, a related question has worried specialists in human reproduction for a decade. They have observed an increase in reproductive problems (a decline in sperm count among men, increasing rates of testicular cancer and sterility, etc). Is that attributable to contamination by the chemical products classified as 'endocrine disruptors' because they disturb the hormonal system? Ever more numerous indicators militate in favour of that conclusion. For example, research published at the beginning of 2006 established the link between exposure to low doses of insecticide and the drop in fertility among the men examined. An additional factor could be atmospheric pollution, which, several studies indicate, affects human reproduction.

More generally, scientists are discussing the links between the contamination of individuals (from the chemicals they absorb from water, food, and the atmosphere) and the constant increase in cancers. Demographers and public health specialists are in fact beginning to envision that the lengthening of life expectancy—one of the most generally acknowledged indicators of human progress—could very soon stop. The average length of human life could even contract. If that were to happen, the causes would be:

- Chemical pollution: "It's only the last thirty years that we have been exposed daily to hundreds of chemicals, the massive production of which dates from the 1970s or 1980s," notes the agronomist Claude Aubert;
- An unbalanced and excessive diet;
- Exposure to atmospheric radioactive and electromagnetic pollution; and
- Too-sedentary habits (television, reliance on the car).

In the United States, women's life expectancy has moved towards a plateau since 1997. And one researcher, Jay Olshansky, reckons that the rapid rise in obesity (two-thirds of adults in the United States are overweight) could soon cause life expectancy in that country to decline.

The Planet No Longer Recovers

One aggravating factor in the planetary environmental crisis is the extraordinary expansion of China—its production having grown at close to 10 percent a year over the last fifteen years—and of India, which has grown at a slightly lower rate. This growth is comparable to that of Japan in the 1960s. Then, the Empire of the

Rising Sun became the world's second largest economy. But with China, a human population ten times that of Japan has entered the economic growth spiral; it therefore weighs more heavily on global ecosystems, notably in its imports of raw materials and wood, the extraction of which affects their environment of origin. For example, China has become the premier global importer of soybeans, stimulating cultivation of that legume in Latin America, which is exacerbating the deforestation of the Amazon rainforest. Asia is also rapidly climbing toward first place in greenhouse gas emissions: in 2004, China emitted 4,707,000,000 tons of carbon gases and India 1,113,000,000 tons, compared to 5,912,000,000 for the United States and 3,506,000,000 for the then fifteen states of the European Union.

China's pressure on the environment—and to a lesser degree, India's—while harmful in itself, cannot excuse that of Western countries: it's because the latter already weigh so heavily on the biosphere that the additional weight of the new powers makes the ecological crisis unbearable. It's not China that poses the problem: it's the fact that it adds to the problems the United States and Europe had already built up. All of us together are beginning to exceed the planet's capacities for recovery. We cut down the forests faster than they can regenerate; we suck up stocks of underground water faster than they can recharge themselves; we emit more greenhouse gases than the biosphere can recycle. Our societies' 'ecological footprint', their environmental impact, according to the concept forged by Swiss expert Mathis Wackernagel, exceeds the planet's 'bio-capacity'. According to Wackernagel, in 1960, humanity used only half of this biological capacity; in 2003, it used 1.2 times that capacity, that is, humanity consumed more environmental resources than the planet produced.

Moreover, the two Asian giants are suffering domestically the perverse effects of their frenetic growth. In China, the loss of arable land to urbanization is extremely rapid (a million hectares per year—after more than twenty-five years' time this loss extends to 7 percent of agricultural acreage). The desert advances more than 100,000 hectares a year, and every year Beijing suffers windstorms from the west. Every spring, the Yellow River is sucked dry for several weeks. Three hundred million Chinese—close to a quarter of the population—drink polluted water, and pollution in the Yangtze, the country's longest river, is becoming so concerning that it threatens the supply of potable water for Shanghai, the country's economic capital. Subterranean water tables are polluted in 90 percent of China's villages, and so are over 70 percent of streams and lakes, according to the official statistics cited by the New China News Agency. Close to one hundred large cities suffer cuts in their water supply every year. Twenty of the thirty cities with the most polluted air in the world are in China. "Chinese air is so saturated with sulphur dioxide that the country has experienced acid rains of a rarely-equalled severity. It is estimated that some 30 percent of arable land suffers from acidification," the Worldwatch Institute reports.

Climate Change, One Aspect of the Global Crisis

To really capture the gravity of the planetary environmental crisis, it is essential to understand that climate change—often presented in an isolated fashion—does not constitute the totality of the crisis. The various environmental disturbances are, in reality, aspects of a single crisis; and climate change is only the most visible facet of the same crisis that the rapid disappearance of biodiversity and the generalized pollution of ecosystems also demonstrate.

Why? Because the three dimensions described here do not constitute autonomous parts of reality. Science considers them separately in order to study them better. But in the reality of the biosphere, they are part of the same phenomenon.

For example, the construction of a highway and its subsequent use will simultaneously impair biodiversity (by fragmenting the ecosystem it crosses), pollute the environment (through emissions of such atmospheric pollutants as nitrogen oxide and particulates, as well as gas spills), and increase carbon-gas emissions by stimulating the traffic of cars and lorries. At the same time, the excess carbon-gas waste leads to an increase in its absorption by the oceans, acidifying them and weakening the ability of coral and plankton to manufacture their calcareous envelope. If nothing changes, the organisms that have a shell of the mineral known as 'aragonite' will have disappeared from the southern oceans by 2030, with harmful consequences to those species that eat them, such as whales and salmon.

In another example of interaction, climate change should favour the spread of vectors of disease beyond their original ecosystems. For example, malaria-bearing mosquitoes will move toward the countries of the Northern Hemisphere. It should also stimulate the erosion of biodiversity: a scientific study published in 2004 estimated that climate change would lead to the disappearance of 35 percent of living species. Although this is probably exaggerated, the study nonetheless suggests the vigour of the connection between the two phenomena.

Conversely, the factors involved in biodiversity destruction frequently affect climate change: close to 20 percent of greenhouse gas emissions are due to deforestation. More generally, the crisis in biodiversity weakens the biosphere's ability to dampen or check greenhouse gas emissions, and consequently it exacerbates their impact.

So we must abandon the idea of separate crises that may be solvable independently of one another. That idea serves special interests only, for example, the nuclear-power lobby, which uses climate change to promote its industry. On the contrary, we must think about the synergy of these crises—their interrelations, their interactions—and accept an unpleasant fact: this synergy is currently working toward a worsening of our state of affairs, with a destructive power that nothing available can temper right now.

The Coming Oil Shock

The environmental crisis is due to human activity, and is the direct consequence of the present economic system. That system could be shaken up by the exhaustion of a part of its energy supplies, a threat that reflects the global crisis affecting our dying civilization: hydrocarbon use is a major source of greenhouse gas and pollution, while its extraction contributes to the destruction of ecosystems with impressive efficiency. The oil crisis was predicted by the so-called Hubbert's Peak theory, named after the U.S. geologist who first formulated it. It asserts that the exploitation of a natural resource follows a bell curve. The summit of that curve corresponds to the time when exploitation reaches a maximum level before declining.

Since the beginning of its use in the nineteenth century, oil has been extracted in increasing quantities at a low cost. But at a certain moment, the cost of extraction continues to go up while production begins to decline. That moment is called the 'peak', or 'Hubbert's Peak'. It does not describe the phase where there's no longer any oil at all, but the one during which people can no longer increase the amount produced and after which the level of production must inexorably decline. That decline, coming at a time when global consumption is continuing to increase, will provoke a significant increase in the price of oil.

The arrival on the oil market of the great emerging countries makes the question of an oil peak a crucial issue. The statistics need no comment: per person, China today consumes one-thirteenth of the oil used in the United States, and India, one-twentieth. If, within the coming decades, the two countries were to reach the present level of consumption in Japan—the most abstemious of the developed countries—they would use 138 million barrels a day. Yet in 2005, global consumption of oil reached 82 million barrels a day.

The peak oil theory is no longer really disputed. Natural gas will follow oil, for the same reasons, with a lag of about fifteen years. The point that is debated is the date when the peak will occur. It was in 2007 for the most pessimistic experts, such as Colin Campbell, one of the geologists who have popularized the theory; it's around 2040 or 2050, even 2060, for the most optimistic. The Total Oil Company, whose best interest, as is true for the entire oil industry, lies in the peak occurring as late as possible, deems that it will happen in 2025. So, when will it happen? It is impossible to know. But the conclusion of expert Jean-Luc Wingert is dead right: "We have entered the 'period of turbulence' that precedes the global Peak and we shall probably never exit from it."

Catastrophe Scenarios

Let me summarize. We have entered a long-term and planetary state of environmental crisis. That crisis is likely to manifest itself through a coming shake-up in the global economic system. Problems that could flare up in an economy approaching saturation and bumping up against the biosphere's limits include a halt in the growth of the U.S. economy, undermined by three giant deficits—the trade deficit, the budget deficit, and domestic indebtedness. Like a junkie who can stay standing only by shooting more heroin, the United States, doped up on hyperconsumption, staggers before it drops.

Another would be a significant slowdown in Chinese growth—since it's known that China cannot possibly sustain the very high pace of annual growth it has experienced. Since 1978, China has experienced annual economic growth of 9.4 percent. Japan is a precedent we shouldn't forget: twenty years of astounding growth, then the long-term stagnation in the beginning of the 1990s. A Chinese crisis would reverberate around the whole world.

It is even possible that no sudden shock will occur, but that the deterioration now underway will continue, in which people will become accustomed, as with a gradual poisoning, to social and environmental dereliction. Apparent respites could come about as a result of the disorder involved. For example, the melting of the Arctic glaciers provoked by global warming could facilitate access to the oil that the polar oceans keep hidden, bringing a breath of oxygen to suffocating economies.

In this last case, people who take ecology seriously imagine other scenarios. Biodiversity specialists are the most cautious. According to Michel Loreau, "For a while, people won't perceive the consequences of the loss of biodiversity. And then, suddenly, catastrophes will occur: new species invasions, the emergence of new diseases; also, for plants, a loss in the productivity of ecosystems." Ecologists think that the destruction of ecosystems will clear the field for harmful organisms that will not be checked by their usual predators, and we could then expect great epidemics. That's how one must understand the fear that avian flu aroused among public health specialists. One of them, Martin McKee, a professor at the London School of Hygiene and Tropical

Medicine, says with respect to the threat of contagious illness: "I cannot even exclude the long-term hypothesis that an unknown organism could appear and wipe out *Homo sapiens*."

In relation to climate and/or oil shock, the projections are more precise. According to Lovelock, as we've seen, wars will increase, destroying civilization. For McKee, "Because of global warming, the habitable regions of the planet will diminish, resulting in population movements unprecedented since the end of the Roman Empire." A Green Party member of the French parliament, Yves Cochet, expects that the sudden arrival of the energy peak will lead to "a brutal increase in the price of transportation: civil aviation would collapse; rural living would be disrupted because of its dependence on the car. The shock would be accompanied by massive unemployment and violent wars for control of Middle East petroleum." Agricultural production would also be affected because of industrialized agriculture's dependence on oil: for tractors, industrial fertilizers, and greenhouse production. Two engineers, Jean-Marc Jancovici and Alain Grandjean, develop a comparable scenario: the decline in oil production results in "a significant recession. Summer droughts increase, drastically reducing grain yields. The energy crisis reduces our adaptive abilities (which are based on cheap and abundant energy). Tropical diseases and flu epidemics increase, but medical infrastructures are overwhelmed, and inequality in care skyrockets."

It is a remarkable fact that these scenarios don't surprise us very much. We can imagine the form that catastrophe will take because we are beginning to experience it on a small scale: the avian flu epidemic prefigures the great epidemics we can imagine; the chaos that followed the flooding of New Orleans in September 2005 is a modest rehearsal for the one that will follow in a continent ravaged by tornados; the heat wave of summer 2003 in Europe is a harbinger of the scorchers to come. In the future, of course, histories will be written that are beyond our current imagination. But our imagination may already reasonably use the limited disasters of today to sketch the face of tomorrow.

However, the most amazing thing of all is that the spectacle is already repeating itself before our eyes, all the indicators—with their unwavering message—are worsening, and our societies still do nothing. For no one can seriously believe that the celebration of 'sustainable development'—which expresses itself through the unrestrained propagation of windmills throughout the landscape, the re-launching of nuclear power, biofuel cultivation, 'socially responsible investments' and the other measures that lobbyists pursue in the quest for new markets—could have any significant impact on the direction in which things are going. 'Sustainable development' is a semantic weapon used to shove aside the dirty word 'ecology'. Moreover, is there any further need to 'develop' France, Germany, or the United States? Let all people of good faith who believe in the virtues of sustainable development ask themselves: Do they observe a slowdown in deforestation? In greenhouse gas emissions? In the paving of the countryside? In the people's use of the car? In the disappearance of species? In water pollution? Some good news—the continuation of the Kyoto Protocol, the restored health of a few wild species, the resurgence of organic agriculture— certainly testifies to the struggles of some and the desire of many to bring about change. But the overall course of things follows the trend, and the trend is in the wrong direction. It is as though we were in 1938 singing, "Everything is going very well . . ."

Sustainable development will be effective if given enough time, some believe. But we no longer have the time: within the next ten years we must reclaim the rudder of the freighter that our irresponsible captains are steering today. The sole function of 'sustainable development' is to maintain profits and avoid the (necessary) change in habits by barely changing course. But it is these profits and these habits that prevent us from changing course. What is the priority? Profits, or the right course?

The Central Question

Here is the central question: while all of this is perfectly clear, why is the system so stubbornly incapable of changing? Several answers come to mind.

One commonly-held view is that, in reality, the situation is not so serious. Even if attentive citizens observe innumerable signals for alarm all around them, the general current of information drowns them in a flood that makes those signals seem relatively minor. There are always cunning 'conservatives', bolstered by their notoriety, who will violently proclaim, using biased arguments, that the alarm is exaggerated. One variant of this theme is to acknowledge the gravity of the problem by asserting that we will be able to adapt almost spontaneously through new technologies.

But one must look further for an explanation. Three factors have the effect of minimizing the impact of the situation.

On the one hand, the dominant framework for explaining the world today is an economic one. Thus, the world enjoys an apparent prosperity marked by the growth in gross domestic product (GDP) and international trade. This description is intrinsically distorted by the fact that this 'economic growth' does not defray the cost of environmental destruction. In accounting terms, a company must reduce the profits from its activities by putting aside sums called 'depreciation' that represent the wear and tear on the capital goods used; thus, when these capital goods are worn out, the company has a reserve available to replace them. But a 'global corporation' does not pay for 'the depreciation of the biosphere', that is, the replacement cost for the natural capital it uses. Although this could have been permissible when the biosphere's absorption capacities were great, such conduct becomes criminal when those possibilities have reached their limit.

Global opinion and decision makers are in the same situation as the head of a business whose accountant has forgotten to factor in depreciation. They think the company is doing well, while it's actually courting bankruptcy.

On the other hand, the leadership elites are ignorant. Trained in economics, engineering, or politics, they are frequently ignorant of science and virtually always lacking the slightest notion of ecology. The habitual reflex of an individual who lacks knowledge about a subject is to neglect, even condemn, those questions that are based on this, in favour of those questions in which he is the most competent. The elites act the same way. Hence, their underestimation of the environmental problem.

A third factor should not be forgotten: the lifestyle of the rich prevents them from sensing what surrounds them. In developed countries, the majority of the population lives in cities, cut off from the environment where the fissures in the biosphere are beginning to show. Moreover, the majority of the population is largely protected from those fissures by the structures of collective management developed in the past; these succeed in dampening the shocks (floods, droughts, earthquakes) when they are not too violent. The average Westerner spends the greater part of his existence in a closed space, going from his car to his air-conditioned office, buying his groceries in a windowless supermarket, dropping his children off in the car, amusing himself at home in an intimate conversation with his television, computer, and so on. The ruling classes, which model opinion, are even further cut off from the social and natural environment: they travel only in cars, live in air-conditioned spaces, and use transportation circuits—airports, business neighborhoods, residential areas—that shelter them from contact with society. Obviously, they disconnect from those problems that they see only through abstract representations.

As for those who are already personally confronted with the social and ecological disasters of the crisis that is underway—the poor in Western urban neighborhoods, African or Chinese peasants, employees in American maquiladoras, slum dwellers everywhere: they have no voice in the issue.

To the question of why nothing changes although it is so obviously imperative that change is needed, a different answer can be given. The collapse of the Soviet Union and the failure of socialism in the 1980s eliminated the possibility of referring to an alternative—or rather, made the idea of an alternative unrealistic. Capitalism profited from its undeniable success over the Soviet Union, while at the same time it was stimulated by the development of microcomputing and digital techniques that played a structural role comparable to that which the development of the railways played in the nineteenth century and the car in the twentieth. It is significant that socialism, the left's centre of gravity, is based on materialism and the nineteenth-century ideology of progress; it has been incapable of integrating the ecological critique. Thus the field is wide open for a single, unequivocal image of the world—one that enjoys its victory over other worldviews and neglects facing up to the new challenges.

But none of these answers, taken alone, is adequate. The answer lies elsewhere, and it encompasses all the others. If nothing happens even as we enter an economic crisis of historic seriousness, it's because the powerful of the world want it that way.

This observation is brutal, and what follows in this book will have to justify it. But that must be one's point of departure; otherwise the precise diagnoses of Al Gore or Lester Brown, not to mention Nicolas Hulot, Jean-Marie Pelt, Hubert Reeves and others who invariably conclude with an appeal to 'humanity', are nothing but sentimental, lukewarm water.

Naïve comrades, there are evil men on Earth.

If one wants to be an ecologist, one must stop being a halfwit.

Ecology totally overlooks social issues, that is, the relationships of power and wealth at the heart of societies.

But similarly, the left overlooks ecology; the left, meaning those for whom the social question—justice—remains primary. Dressed in what remains of the rags of Marxism, the left incessantly repaints the pictures of the nineteenth century, or sinks into the 'realism of 'tempered (free-market) liberalism'. Thus, the social crisis—marked by the deepening of inequality and by the dissolution of the connections, both private and collective, of solidarity—that seems to overlie the ecological crisis, serves *de facto* to brush it aside from our field of vision.

Consequently, we find simple-minded ecologists—ecology with no social conscience—alongside a left stuck in the old days—social conscience with no ecology; and above them all, the happy capitalists: 'Speak, good people, and, above all, remain divided.'

We must get out of this space and understand that the ecological crisis and the social crisis are two faces of the same disaster. This disaster is implemented by a system of power that has no other objective than to maintain the privileges of the ruling classes.

2 | ENVIRONMENTAL CRISIS, SOCIAL CRISIS

The big Guatemala City dump is not far from the centre of town. It's simply called *Relleno Sanitario*—the garbage pit. The road that leads there subtly changes character the closer you get: bags of salvaged material begin to appear in front of several stores; you see people go by with bags of rubbish; houses become scarcer, and then you pass between two cement walls. The walls stop, and there you are. It's an immense quarry, progressively filled in with garbage, piled to the top and pushing along into a narrow and luxuriant valley. Our little truck slowly descends the winding road following a garbage truck. The scene is crowded and colourful, girded by cliffs and slums constructed on a slope. Dozens of yellow trucks—and some horse-drawn wagons—are emptied by hand onto earth stippled with every colour of plastic—green, blue, yellow dots. An unpleasant smell hovers. On this plain of garbage and earth pushed by several bulldozers, hundreds of men, women, and children rummage, rake, fill up bags, or sit talking together. Dogs wander here and there, while black birds fly in the azure sky or pace the ground in groups. The dump is several acres large. In a corner stand shacks made of wood, plastic sheeting, and corrugated sheet metal; there is an impromptu bar—one may dine there—as well as some shops, and a few residents who are staying at home. Sometimes meat is found in the trucks. Who knows?—maybe it will be served at the bar.

So the dump pushes into the valley through which the Rio Baranco snakes, about thirty metres below the piled-up garbage that progressively fills it in. An asphyxiated, polluted former stream, it no longer collects anything but the juice the mountain of filth oozes in abundance when it rains. Thus does the rotten mountain spread, following the course of the poisoned stream.

Araceli and Gamaliel are a woman and man, each about thirty years old. They have been working there for two years, and live 20 kilometres away. Together they earn 35 quetzals a day (roughly £2.50). They have no specialty; they gather up a little of whatever they can and re-sell it to the tradesmen who are positioned on the dump. Those tradesmen will go and sell off their pickings at the city's biggest market, located near the bus station. When it rains, work is impossible. Araceli and Gamaliel eat only a little, food they've prepared at home. He was a mechanic in Nicaragua. The boss didn't want to pay him; he left. He has no papers, but the police don't come here. Araceli has four children. She babysat other people's children and lost her position. She chose this work to survive.

Christian, from Doctors without Borders, tells me that *guajiros* (peasants) have lots of respiratory complaints. But our little group is drawing stares; we'd better go. We drive to a valley not far from the dump, where a little town has grown up on the unpaved ground of another garbage depot that reached saturation. People had no houses, Mateo Suretnoj relates, until five families got together to organize the invasion on 14th October 1999. They were, for the most part, *guajiros* working on the dump—at 35 quetzals a day, it was impossible to pay for lodging. The police did not react, and the mayor let them move in. They came with nothing but plastic sheeting. Little by little, they built shacks, and the 'October 14 Community' now numbers close to five hundred souls. The children go to school. At 10 p.m., the community is locked up. The municipality has installed a water pipe and, in the last few months, electricity. Several roads have been cemented onto the tamped-down ground. In every house, a tube is planted 50 centimetres deep to remove the fermentation gases that form in the underlying filth. Cypress and magnolias have been planted to fight against erosion. But the ground labours, and fissures appear on the low walls.

That was November 2001. I was on my way back from reporting on a famine in the hills of the Guatemalan wilderness and on the still-unhealed wounds from Hurricane Mitch, which had swept through Central America two years before. I had fallen, if one may use that expression, into this universe of poverty in the rubbish heap of the capital, Guatemala City, itself steeped in despair and violence. These several hours in the dump seemed to me to deserve a more in-depth report. But in Paris, my connection at the paper told me in a somewhat annoyed tone that it wasn't a very original topic.

In fact, the paper had only very rarely reported about people living in dumps, for there was nothing new about the fact that in the planet's four corners—in Manila, in Cairo, in Mexico, and in practically all the capitals of Latin America—thousands of the destitute confront the shit, the disease, and the indignity of picking through garbage to earn a few cents.

Poverty is so widespread that it has become banal. And there wasn't anything particularly piquant to say about Guatemala City. Nothing especially interesting to describe at Fatai-Karma, one village among many similar in Niger. There men talk about the drought, the necessary departure of youth 'in flight', the days of scarcity when nothing is left at all: "Then only death remains," says one man, and everyone laughs. Nothing particularly original about those guys who beg for alms in Saskatoon, a rich city in the Canadian West, on a winter night when the thermometer hits minus fifteen Celsius. None of this excites the interest of the residents of the planet's great cities very much. They regard it wearily, without paying it any further attention.

Hold on—here's another of the innumerable maps of poverty,

the one traced by my morning itinerary on the way to work in Paris. On the Rue de Buzenval, when the post office opens, a gypsy holds the door for the people, selling *L'Itinerant* (The Vagabond), a newspaper sold by the homeless. On the other side of the street, in a corner of the wall, three men in their early thirties take their places during the morning for an interminable palaver washed down with bottles of beer and rosé wine. At the entrance to the subway, a woman with short gray hair intermittently begs. I get off at the Rue de Montreuil, then Rue du Faubourg-Saint-Antoine, without encountering any more poor wretches—but if I were to go right, to the corner of the Rue Faideherbe and the Rue de Chanzy, I would encounter one of the tents, distributed since the winter of 2005 by Doctors of the World, that give the homeless the semblance of a roof. Turning onto the Avenue Ledru-Rollin, I discover the destitute on a corner of the bridge that leads to the Quai d'Austerlitz: a group has established itself there the last few months. They are rather young men, who call out to passers-by during the day, imploring them to leave an offering in the jam jar tied to the end of a stick with a string: they fish for coins. On the other side of the square, in front of the bus stop, a Metro grate exhales a cloud of warmth. It is unusual for there not to be a man stretched out there, with no blanket, sleeping on the grille, two steps from the racket and the exhaust of this spot's intense traffic. On the Rue Buffon, across from the Jardin des Plantes, men often doze in sleeping bags at the entrance of a building which is set back from the street and forms an inviting nook. Less comfortable, the grilles of cellar windows further up the street on the right, are sometimes occupied by vagabonds, with no other mattress than a sheet of cardboard. Earlier, there also used to be a kid in the area who checked out the garbage cans before the garbage truck got there, but I haven't seen him for a long time. The next milestone on this track of misfortune that my bicycle skims through is on the Rue Broca, where, under the bridge of the Boulevard de Port-Royal, a quasi-house has been rigged up: it's a bedroom without walls, furnished with a big mattress, a staved-in sofa, and a heterogeneous collection of plastic bags, cardboard sheets, and shopping carts full of found objects. I arrive at the newspaper where I am employed. Not long ago, two bums had installed an improbable shack beneath the overhead Metro where they spent their days in the middle of a pile of objects that mimicked a solid home. The big bad wolf must have passed by and huffed and puffed very hard at the house of wisps; there's no longer anything there. I am certain that, like me, my journalist colleagues said to themselves, with some internal twinge, that there was a little story to be told, a sketch that says much about the world. But there, right under our eyes, too easy, too ordinary. Poverty. The poor. Et cetera.

The Return of Poverty

Emotion—or empathy—draws only a partial picture. Statistics complete the illustration. "In the course of the winter of 2005–06, shelters for the homeless were confronted with an increase in demand in 54 departments," France's minister for social cohesion announced in April 2006. More and more people in France live in trailers, perhaps hundreds of thousands. In the world, there are more than 120 million children living by themselves, according to United Nations' Children's Fund (UNICEF) and the International Labor Organization (ILO). "In 2004 in France, close to 3.5 million people received means-tested benefits, or an increase of 3.4 percent over the previous year. The number receiving RMI [*revenu minimum d'insertion*, French welfare payments] (€425 for singles, €638 for couples) jumped 8.5 percent to reach

1.2 million. The main victims: singles, single-parent families, and youth," the minister announced.

According to the National Observatory of Poverty and Social Exclusion (ONPES), the poor numbered close to 3.7 million in France in 2003, but that number was 7 million (or 12.4 percent of the population) according to the European definition. What is the usual definition of poverty? It's an income threshold: a single person in France who earns less than 50 percent of the median income is poor. The median income is the figure that divides the population in two: half the people earn more than that income, the other half less. At the beginning of 2006, the poverty threshold was €1,254 (£1,000 as at September 2008) a month; that figure is after taxes and includes public transfer payments such as family allowances. The level is then adjusted according to the number of people per household: each additional adult and every child over fourteen counts for an additional half share; each child under 14 for 30 percent of a share. For example, the median monthly income for a couple with two children under the age of 14 is €2,633 (£2,100); a family constituted this way will be called poor if its monthly income is less than half that figure, or €1,316 (£1,050). The European Union definition follows the same approach but fixes the poverty threshold at 60 percent of the median income.

In Switzerland, the Caritas association deemed the number of poor in 2005 to be a million persons, or 14 percent of the population; in 2003, they numbered 850,000; as for indigents—those devoid of any means—they make up 6 percent of the Swiss population. In Germany, the proportion of people living below the poverty threshold went from 12.1 percent of the population in 1998 to 13.5 percent of the population in 2003. In Great Britain, it reached 22 percent in 2002. In the United States, 23 percent of the population earns less than half the median income (that is, is poor by the French definition of poverty). In Japan, "the number of households with no savings doubled in five years to reach 25 percent. . . . The number of households depending on social assistance increased by a third to reach one million."

Are the poor lazy? No. Having a salaried job does not protect people from destitution anymore. "One-third of homeless people in the capital state that they are employed," one discovers, while several dozen employees of the Paris municipality have themselves lost their lodgings. As economist Jacques Rigaudiat explains, "With the rise in CDD [contracts of a specified duration], temporary work, and now the CNE [the new employee contract that provides reduced security], we are experiencing a dislocation in the traditional forms of employment status." The ONPES confirms this: "The precarious character of a growing number of jobs and the meagreness of some salaries lead people who have nonetheless worked all year long into situations of poverty." The phenomenon is anything but negligible: Pierre Concialdi, a researcher at the Institute for Economic and Social Research (IRES), reports, "According to the official thresholds and statistical sources, there are between 1.3 and 3.6 million poor workers in France. Everything suggests that this phenomenon has grown in recent years." The development is the same in other countries, such as Germany. According to Labor Minister Franz Müntefering, "300,000 full-time employees earn so little money, they have to turn to social assistance."

The experts argue over whether poverty is on the rise. According to the Alarm Network on Inequalities, which publishes the BIP 40 (Barometer of Inequality and Poverty), integrating about 60 indicators other than monetary income alone, "the rise in poverty and inequality has been continuing for twenty years." The French Institute for Economic Statistics (INSEE) deems, however, that the level of poverty has slightly decreased between 1998 and 2002. But there is a consensus that after several decades of regression, poverty is no longer diminishing. "There's been a switch in the trend," summarizes Louis Maurin, director of the Observatory of Inequalities.

On top of that, poverty is no longer a domain separate from society, a well-delineated and unfortunate hell: the whole social body is being dragged into a cycle of vulnerability. "The borders of poverty are becoming blurred," observes Martin Hirsch, president of Emmaüs France. "There are not, on the one hand, the poor who correspond strictly to the statistical definition of the term, and, on the other, 90 percent of the population safe from poverty. On the contrary, we observe diffusion in the factors of precariousness, forming a sort of great halo of vulnerability around the population whose resources are superior to the threshold of monetary poverty." For Jacques Rigaudiat, it is also more relevant to talk about precariousness than poverty: "A quarter to a third of the population lives in a precarious situation. Consequently there are overall close to twenty million people concerned, that is, households earning less than 1.7 or 1.8 times the SMIC [minimum wage]." Twenty million people: a third of the French population.

The Globalization of Poverty

If the developed countries are rediscovering poverty, it remains very present in the countries of the Southern Hemisphere. "A billion people survive in absolute poverty on less than a dollar a day," notes the United Nations Development Program (UNDP); another billion make do on less than $2 a day. It is also estimated that 1.1 billion people are without potable water and that 2.4 billion don't have proper sanitation.

It would, however, be fallacious to present a picture of general impoverishment. Life expectancy is increasing in the countries of the south, which is an incontestable improvement, while extreme poverty has receded, declining from 28 percent of the global population in 1990 to 21 percent today.

The importance of China, and, to a lesser extent, of India, weighs heavily in this planetary development. The growth of the two Asian giants has induced an increase in the average wealth of their populations, which the reduction in the number of the poor reflects: "The share of the population living on under a dollar a day fell from 66 percent in China around 1980 to 17 percent in 2001." Similarly, China has reduced the number of its citizens who suffer from hunger by 58 million.

But on the global scale, progress has slowed down a great deal: "Since the mid-1990s, poverty measured by the dollar-a-day threshold has declined five times more slowly than between 1980 and 1996." Similarly, hunger is no longer receding. The Food and Agriculture Organization (FAO) report on food insecurity in 2003 surprised observers: while the number of the starving in the world had steadily decreased for several decades, it began to increase again from 1995–97. The number of residents of under-developed countries not eating enough to satisfy their hunger was estimated at 800 million in the 2003 report, while 2 billion human beings suffer food shortages. Even India is seeing the number of its undernourished citizens (221 million) increasing again, and China is failing to reduce its number (142 million) any further. "This development," one of the organization's experts, Henri Josserand, explained in Rome, "reflects the increase in poverty. Certainly agricultural production in the world is growing faster than the population, and there is enough for everyone to eat. But the poor are ever more numerous and lack the means to access regular nourishment." More recent statistics confirm that the situation is worsening. In September 2008, the FAO reported that the number of undernourished people has reached 925 million.

In fact, at the global level, social machinery has broken down. The general growth in monetary wealth now translates into progress in the material conditions of existence for the great mass of the population only with difficulty. One striking indicator of that is the extent of urban poverty: urbanization is no longer what it had been up until now, a way for peasants to improve their lot by fleeing the poverty of the countryside. Not only do a billion of the world's city dwellers (out of three billion) live in slums, notes the United Nations agency responsible for habitat, but poverty is becoming "a major and expanding characteristic of urban life." People flee rural scarcity but find themselves in the city in hovels with neither water nor electricity, ogling insecure jobs in the permanent uncertainty of the immediate future. And they frequently do so with an empty belly.

The Rich Are Still Richer

There is no necessary connection between poverty and inequality. But these days, the increase in poverty reflects the increase in inequalities, as much within societies as between groups of nations.

In France, according to INSEE, "the average gross income of the most well-to-do 20 percent of households remains 7.4 times that of the poorest 20 percent. The gap diminishes to 3.8 once the fiscal charges (direct and indirect taxes) that some pay and the different public allocations and assistance that others receive are counted in." Pierre Concialdi of the Institute of Social and Economic Research (IRES) notes that "for the last twenty years, average wage conditions have deteriorated: wages are far from having increased at the same rate as growth. The tendency is the same for social allowances. In parallel, the purchasing power of the incomes from capital has tripled since the end of the 1980s."

This stretching of the scale of inequalities is found throughout the Western world. For economist Thomas Piketty, since 1970, "inequality has only truly increased in the United States and the United Kingdom, but, at the very least, inequality in salaries in all countries stopped declining during the 1980s." In fact, a study conducted by Piketty and Emmanuel Saez shows that, starting in the 1990s in the United States, Canada, and Great Britain, inequality regained the very high levels that preceded the Second World War: the richest tenth of the population takes away 40 percent of total income, while its share had previously been stable at around 32 percent since 1954.

In the United States, summarizes the *Economist*, "income inequality has reached levels not seen since the 1880s. . . . According to Washington research firm the Economic Policy Institute, between 1979 and 2000 real household income for the poorest fifth of the population grew 6.4 percent, while that of households in the upper fifth increased 70 percent. . . . In 1979, the average income of the top 1 percent was 133 times that of the bottom 20 percent; in 2000, that ratio reached 189." "Inequality has grown regularly for thirty years," thrills the conservative magazine *Forbes*, which incidentally thereby signalled that the presidencies of Democrats Jimmy Carter and Bill Clinton changed nothing in that fundamental tendency.

In Japan up until the beginning of the 1990s, journalist Philippe Pons notes, "the majority of Japanese thought they belonged to a vast middle class. This perception has exploded into bits." At this time, "inequalities have begun to widen, following the collapse of the financial bubble. . . . The gap in incomes has widened among the younger generation (twenty- to thirty-year-olds) because of the growing precariousness and fragmentation of the job market due to the growth in temporary and part-time work. . . . Along with an upper class which surfs the wave of the recovery, another class has been created at the same time, one that is dragged down: households of intermediate income—the principal victims of the recession—have seen their standard of living decline."

Everywhere, purchasing power has fallen behind productivity gains, unlike what happened between 1945 and 1975. And social situations are congealing: "In the middle of the 1950s," writes Louis Maurin, "executives earned four times more than workers on average, but workers could hope to catch up with the average executive salary of 1955 by around 1985, given the rhythm of salary progression. In the mid-1990s, executives earned 'only' 2.6 times the average worker salary, but workers needed three centuries before they could hope to reach that level"; one earns much less than others, which is bearable, but one has lost any hope of catching up, which is far less so. Social mobility has broken down.

A new inequality between generations results from this: the members of the middle and more humble classes are discovering that they cannot guarantee their children a higher standard of living than their own. The assets and income of adults over the age of forty to fifty are at a distinctly higher level than those of younger adults. The poor are not the same people as they were twenty years ago, notes sociologist Louis Chauvel: "Once, it was old people who were going to die soon. Today, the poor are above all the young, who have a long future of poverty to look forward to."

Observing income alone prettifies the general picture; it's also necessary to study assets, which statisticians capture less well than they do income. The disparities in capital are far greater than salary and income inequalities. "If, with respect to purchasing power, the relationship between the richest 10 percent and the poorest 10 percent of the population is four to one according to INSEE's income statistics, it goes to 64 to 1 when the value of assets owned is taken into account! And further," continues the newspaper *Marianne*, "for the least wealthy, one has to count durable goods such as scooters to not end up with a ratio that tends toward the infinite." The income from this capital profits the richest first. The inequality of assets leads to a concrete inequality much greater than that indicated by the inequality of incomes.

Birth of the Global Oligarchy

In the majority of non-Western countries, inequality is often greater still. In Guatemala in 1997, for example, 20 percent of the population earned 61 percent of the national income. Generally, Latin America and Africa have much more unequal social structures than do Asian and the developed countries. But in Asia, as in the rich countries, inequality is gaining ground. In India, the country's growing wealth "is not accompanied by a spectacular decline in poverty," the UNDP notes. In China, reports the monthly *Alternatives economiques*, "the Communist Party's response [to the 1989 student rebellion] consisted of accelerating economic development, all the while strengthening its control in every domain: in politics, the media, law, and economics. Suddenly, an oligarchy established itself in which the Communist dictatorship's political and governmental power was associated with an economic power that was ever more openly capitalist and oriented toward personal and private wealth accumulation, without worrying about the situation of society's castoffs, whose situation continued to deteriorate. In barely thirty years, China has thus become one of the most unequal countries on the planet." A Chinese boss, Zhang Xin, from the real estate firm Soho China, confirms the analysis: "The greatest challenge facing China is income disparity. The highest incomes keep growing faster all the time, while the mass of the population is still trying to satisfy basic needs."

Finally, one must remember the immense gap that exists between rich countries and poor countries. According to the UNDP, that gap is no longer decreasing for such indicators as life expectancy, infant mortality, and literacy. Not only have the poorest countries "not been able to reduce their poverty, but they get further and further behind rich countries. Measured at the extremes, the gap between the average citizen of the richest countries and the average citizen of the poorest is immense and continues to expand. In 1990, the average American was 38 times richer than the average Tanzanian. Today, he is 61 times as rich."

The inequality between the countries of the North and the countries of the South is taking another form. China's rapid development—like India's, Brazil's, and others'—is taking place at a huge environmental cost. Certainly, during the nineteenth and twentieth centuries, Europe and the United States also grew rapidly at the price of enormous pollution and the massive transformation of their environments. The big emerging countries are following the path of their predecessors. But the latter benefited from an essential resource: the environmental dampener constituted by the rest of the biosphere to absorb their pollution. That wealth is no longer available to the countries of the South, and the ecological limit is going to bridle their expansion prematurely. The South "cannot dampen the negative effects of growth, and that is a mortal difficulty," writes Sunita Narain, director of the Centre for Science and the Environment in New Delhi, India.

To Reduce Poverty, Diminish the Rich

With respect to this summary picture of global poverty and inequality, it's important to make two observations.

In the first place, poverty is not an absolute state. One understands that better through recourse to another definition of it, adopted by the Council of Europe in 1984: The poor are "those persons, families, and groups of persons whose resources (material, cultural, and social) are so limited as to exclude them from the minimum acceptable way of life in the Member State to which they belong." That is to say that poverty is always relative: a poor person in the United States today is undoubtedly richer than a serf in the Middle Ages or a miner of the Jack London era; he is also richer than a young unemployed person in La Paz or Niamey. For example, Mateo, from the Guatemala City slum, would probably love to have the trailer that the Toulouse labourer in dire financial straits sees as a symbol of his degradation.

Within the heart of a given society, one is poor, first of all, because one is much less wealthy than the rich. This relativism of poverty, which takes the form of an apparent truism—a person is poor because he is not rich—has a crucial consequence: it means that a reduction in inequality (within a given society as well as on a planetary scale) reduces poverty.

That observation, which defies common sense, must be completed by another remark: a policy aiming to reduce inequality would also seek to strengthen the collective services that are independent of each person's income. In fact, it is generally true that the more unequal a society is, the less guaranteed are collective services. For example, in the United States, which is the most unequal Western country, "health care expenses account for 14 percent of GNP (versus 10.3 percent in the Netherlands and in France)," notes André Cicolella. "Close to 60 million Americans have no health insurance, administrative costs are 14 percent (versus 5 percent in France)," while "the indicators of health, according to the WHO, place the United States in 37th place globally, far behind European countries, as well as behind Costa Rica and the Sultanate of Oman." Consequently, improvement in collective services would produce an improvement in the material situation of the poor. One imagines that such an improvement would come about through a transfer of a part of the resources of the richest people toward services useful to all.

The Forgotten Poverty: Environmental Destitution

A second observation follows: poverty is linked to environmental degradation. The poor live in the most polluted places, in proximity to industrial areas, close to transport lines, in neighborhoods poorly serviced in water supply or garbage collection. One way of apprehending poverty in other than monetary terms would thus be through a description of the environmental conditions of existence. On top of that, it is the poor who primarily suffer the impact of the environmental crisis: in China, warns Environment Minister Zhou Shenxian, "the environment has become a social issue that stimulates social contradictions." He indicates that in 2004, the country experienced 51,000 conflicts related to the environment. Among them, one counts, for example, dozens of 'cancer villages' bordered by chemical factories that shamelessly spew pollutants into the air and water, causing serious disease among their impotent neighbours. Similarly, conflicts connected to the theft of peasants' lands to feed unbridled real estate speculation are also increasing: 74,000 in 2004 as compared with 58,000 in 2003. Conflict over land appropriation leads to bloody clashes (6 peasants were killed by the police in June 2005, and 20 in December 2005).

Those are not events limited solely to China. Real estate conflicts are violent in Brazil (39 murders in 2004). Climate change is affecting the peasants of the Sahel first. The spread of soy cultivation in Latin America is occurring in large part at the expense of small farmers. Natural catastrophes—floods, hurricanes, tidal waves—strike the poor all the more violently in that they have fewer means to protect themselves and no insurance for restoration.

"In numerous cases," the experts of Millennium Ecosystem Assessment observe,

> it is the poor who suffer from the loss of environmental services due to the pressure exerted on natural systems for the benefit of other communities, often in other parts of the world. For example, dams chiefly benefit the cities they supply with water and electricity, while rural residents may lose access to the submerged land and to fishing. Deforestation in Indonesia or in the Amazon is partially stimulated by demand for wood, paper, and agricultural products from regions far distant from the exploited areas, while it is the indigenous people who suffer from the disappearance of forest resources. The impact of climate change will be felt above all in the poorest parts of the world—for example, as it exacerbates drought and reduces the agricultural production of the driest regions—while greenhouse gas emissions essentially come from rich populations.

Moreover, agriculture connects poverty and the environmental crisis. At the global level, poverty concerns mostly peasants: two-thirds of those who subsist on a dollar a day or less live in rural areas. The implicit choice of economic powers across the planet is to consider that the question will be settled by the rural exodus, as poor peasants are supposed to be able to find the resources procured by industrial development in the city. The weakness of agricultural policies favours bad land management, erosion of the land, and then its being abandoned. Peasants, in the end, leave their villages. Now, as we have seen, the city is no longer the place for the promised prosperity. The scrawny peasant's steps are leading him to the destitution of the slums.

But it's not only the absence of agricultural policies that breeds this situation. Competition in global markets from Northern agri-business—overequipped and able to produce almost a hundred tons of grain per full-time employee a year at low cost—with farmers lacking adequate resources and producing less than a ton per person per year leads to impoverishment, bankruptcy, and the exodus of the poor farmers. In fact, as agronomist Marc Dufumier notes, "what some call 'free trade' is nothing other than putting farmers whose conditions of productivity are extremely unequal into competition." That imbalance is all the more absurd in that the strong productivity of Northern agriculture is obtained at the price of significant ecological damage—excessive water consumption, the spreading of harmful pesticides, and massive utilization of fertilizers provoking water eutrophication or pollution by nitrates.

Overall, poverty and the environmental crisis are inseparable. Just as there is a synergy between different ecological crises, there is a synergy between the global environmental crisis and the social crisis: they respond to one another, influence one another, and deteriorate in tandem.

3 | THE POWERFUL OF THIS WORLD

The dictionary defines *oligarchy* as "1: government by the few 2: a government in which a small group exercises control, esp. for corrupt and selfish purposes; also: a group exercising such control." Today, the planet is ruled by an oligarchy that accumulates income, assets, and power with a zeal for greed not seen since the U.S. 'robber barons' at the end of the nineteenth century.

Between 2000 and 2004, the remuneration of the bosses at the forty largest companies quoted on the French Stock Exchange—the so-called CAC 40—doubled to an average of €2.5 million annually. If one includes the stock options (the ability to buy shares at an advantageous price) they enjoy, the figure reaches €5.6 million in 2004, according to the consulting firm Proxinvest, or over €15,000 a day. Thus, in 2005, the best-paid bosses in France pocketed: €22.6 million (Lindsay Owen-Jones of L'Oréal); €16.3 million (Bernard Arnault, LVMH); €13.7 million (Jean-René Fourtou of Vivendi); and so on. Arnaud Lagardère (Lagardère SCA) was—not counting stock options—the best paid, at €7 million. We have to go down to the 79th boss listed by Capital to get below the threshold of €1 million (£800,000 in September 2008) in annual salary.

Company heads are not the only ones to enjoy the manna. Since 1998, the remuneration for the 435 board members of CAC 40 companies climbed 215 percent according to Proxinvest, while French salaries overall during the same period rose only 25 percent.

In addition to salary and stock options, it is often the case that our friends the bosses receive a welcome gift when they join a company—two years of salary—as well as a departure bonus, a retirement umbrella that is 40 percent of salary—for example, €1.2 million a year paid to Daniel Bernard of Carrefour—paid expenses, a company credit card, meals, a chauffeur, a tax consultant, attendance allowances for participation on other companies' boards of directors, and so on. These boards of directors are a custom that allows the executive tribe to strengthen its connections. The attendance allowances add an amenity to the joy of meeting again; in 2004, they averaged €34,500.

France is not alone in pampering its bosses. In 2005, according to a Standard and Poor's study, the average remuneration for the CEOs of the 500 largest companies in the United States rose to 430 times that of the average worker—ten times more than in 1980. The Sunoco boss, John Drosdick, received $23 million a year; the AT&T boss, Edward Whitacre, $17 million; U.S. Steel's John Surma, $6.7 million; Alcoa's Alain Belda, $7.5 million. Leaving these companies is an opportunity to carry away a bundle of money. In December 2005, Lee Raymond, CEO for Exxon, the world's biggest oil company, was able to salve the sorrow of his departure with a $400 million package. The Occidental petroleum boss settled for $135 million over three years. Richard Fairbank, Capital One Financial CEO, outperformed him at $249 million when he exercised his stock options in 2004.

In France, departure gifts are less cushy, but not entirely small potatoes. Daniel Bernard, Carrefour CEO, left in April 2005 with severance pay of €38 million, to which were added 0.6 percent of capital as stock options, or another €170 million. De Vinci CEO Antoine Zacharias left that company in January 2006 with a €13 million bonus to help him forget his 2005 annual salary of €4.3 million that a cushion of €170 million completed. Jean-Marc Espalioux, president of the Accor board of directors, left in January 2006 with €12 million. Igor Landau (Aventis), who lost the IPO Sanofi threw him, also pocketed €12 million. Havas parted from Alain de Pouzilhac with €7.8 million.

In 1989, Peugeot CEO Jacques Calvet created a scandal when he treated himself to a 46 percent salary increase over two years— at 2.2 million francs (€330,000) he earned more than 30 times the salary of an employee in his company. Today, his CAC 40 colleagues earn more than 100 times more than a minimum-wage employee. In 2000, *Le Monde* reported, the "management guru Peter Drucker" warned: "Thirty years ago, the highest multiplier between a company's average salary and its highest salary was 20. Now, we are closing in on 200. It's extremely pernicious. The banker J. P. Morgan, whom we know liked money very much, had a fixed rule that top management should not have a salary exceeding twenty times the average. That rule was very wise. Today, there's an inordinate attention paid to income and wealth. That totally destroys the spirit of teamwork." Mr. Drucker may be a 'guru', but the executives did not listen to him.

The most startling thing in this "bacchanalia," to use *Forbes's* expression, is that it's not the employees or the Left hotly protesting this organized hold-up, but the shareholders and investors who recognize that this upward distribution of corporate revenues is occurring at their expense.

The Global Sect of Greedy Gluttons

Yet the shareholders and the speculators who live off the market don't do so badly. Between 1995 and 2005, income from dividends grew 52 percent in France, according to an investigation by the weekly *Marianne*; over the same period, the median salary increased 7.8 percent, or seven times less. At the beginning of

2006, the French press observed the rise in profits distributed to shareholders by the CAC 40 companies: +33 percent. Chagrined intellects compared that figure to the average rise in employee purchasing power: +1.6 percent. "This profit is not the result of any risk taking, of any entrepreneurial behavior. It's a rent, obtained with no effort," commented Robert Rochefort in *La Croix*.

The officials of finance also accumulate tidy little sums: at the end of 2005, *Le Monde* related, "3,000 of the City's [London's] bankers will have a bonus of over a million pounds." The investment banking firm Goldman Sachs, which pulled off three of the biggest company mergers of 2005, distributed $21.3 billion dollars to its 22,425 employees, or $912,000 on average per employee. Greenwich, Connecticut, near New York, the hedge fund homeland, is a place where an income of less than a million dollars makes you "the plankton at the bottom of the economic food chain," notes the *Financial Times*.

Other individuals, gambling on company creation, the market, mergers, and so on, become billionaires. "In 1988, a man with $150 million dollars was considered rich," says Philip Beresford, who establishes the list of the five thousand richest Britons every year. "Today, it's more like one and a half billion!" The increasing number of billionaires in the world is striking: in 1985, when *Forbes* magazine began its census, it counted 140 of them; in 2002, they were 476; in 2005, 793. Together, these 793 individuals possessed $2.6 trillion, a sum equal to "the entirety of developing countries' foreign debt," according to the Committee for the Cancellation of Third World Debt (CADTM). Another way of looking at it is to observe, as does the United Nations Development Program, that the income of the world's 500 richest people exceeds that of the 416 million poorest people in the world. One ends up getting lost in all these figures, but here's a big one: one hyper-rich person has more than do a million of his fellow human beings put together.

There are even more amazing facts. The news is not much noised about, perhaps in a little column at the bottom of a page in *Le Monde*, but there are people who earn more than $1 billion a year. Yes—not their capital, but their income, really, $1 billion. I had trouble believing what I read, written by my colleague Cécile Prudhomme, who unearthed this extravagant news. She showed me the hard-to-find document that inventories the hit parade of the winners of this unbelievable lottery, the managers of the 'best' American speculative funds: James Simons of Renaissance Technologies and T. Boone Pickens of BP Capital Management were enriched in this manner during 2005 by $1.5 and $1.4 billion dollars, respectively, while George Soros had to make do with $840 million. On average, in 2005, each of the managers of the best paid of these funds earned $363 million, an increase of 45 percent over 2004.

The sect of the hyper-rich has no country. *Forbes* counts 33 billionaires in Russia, 8 in China, and 10 in India. And of the 8.7 million millionaires on the planet according to the Merrill Lynch and Capgemini study, 2.4 million are in Asia, 300,000 in Latin America, and 100,000 in Africa.

In the poorest countries, the caste is composed of those at the apex of the state connected to Western elites: the local ruling classes have negotiated their participation in planetary predation by their ability either to make natural resources accessible to multinational corporations or to assure social order. In the countries of the former Soviet Union, a financial oligarchy formed itself alongside government structures through the appropriation of the spoils of the state. As one Russian commentator observed, "This massive wealth accumulation in several hands was not so much obtained through successes in the domain of production, but rather by a constant redistribution of collective wealth from the bottom to the top, through the reduction of taxes on the rich and the distribution of new privileges to the business sector, all effected while destroying the social mechanisms created after the Second World War."

In Asia, the oligarchy also flourishes on the development of local economies by accommodating, particularly in China, an extreme exploitation of workers and despoliation of the peasantry.

The global oligarchy likes to protect its fortune in fiscal paradises, safe havens where taxation of inheritances, wealth, and other assets is reduced to a symbolic level. Tax evasion, moreover, is one of the rules of good management: "Lakshmi Mittal [CEO of the ArcelorMittal steel group] lives in London," *Paris-Match* relates. His group is incorporated in Holland, while his family holdings are based in Luxembourg, the Canaries, and the Virgin Islands. "Nothing unusual in that," retorts a Mittal spokesperson. "That structure responds to fiscal optimization concerns. The Arcelor Group also uses tax havens. It even has subsidiaries incorporated in the Cayman Islands."

Tax havens are a useful means to exert pressure on governments to reduce taxation of the rich. In Germany, employers convinced Chancellor Gerhard Schroeder to suppress the 52 percent taxation of capital gains on shareholding sales. In Japan, the top tax rate on income went from 70 percent to 37 percent during the 1990s; Prime Minister Junichiro Koizumi added a reduction in the inheritance tax on top of that. In France, the fiscal reform that went into effect in 2007 grants €80 of tax relief to a minimum-wage earner, but €10,000 to someone who earns €20,000 a month. According to the French Observatory of Economic Cycles (OFCE), no less than 70 percent of the €3.5 billion in planned tax reductions will go into the pockets of only 20 percent of taxpayers. In the United States, President George

Bush has implemented the 'compassion' that was one of his 2000 campaign slogans: the tax reductions begun in 2001 represent $1.9 trillion over ten years. According to a study by the Urban Institute, a left-leaning organization, the reduction of taxes on dividends has allowed those who earn more than $1 million a year to save $42,000 over that period, but those who earn between $10,000 and $20,000 save only $2.

"If there is no justice," wrote Saint Augustine, "what are kingdoms, if not vast hold-ups?"

Bolting the Château Doors

The opulent class is becoming a separate caste of society that reproduces itself *sui generis* through the transmission of networks of wealth, privilege and power. Thus, in France, for example, hereditary capitalism is reconstituting itself, updating the expression in vogue between the two World Wars, the '200 families'. Among the Lagardères, Jean-Luc has transmitted capital and power to his son Arnaud. François Pinault hands the reins over to François-Henri. With salutary obstinacy, the Michelin and Peugeot tribes keep their companies inside the familial boundaries. Patrick Ricard manages the company his father founded, as does Martin Bouygues, son of Francis, and Vincent Bolloré, the heir to a stationers' dynasty founded in 1861. Gilles Pélisson is at the head of Accor thanks to his uncle, Gérard. Vianney Mulliez, nephew to Gérard Mulliez, the president of Auchan, is taking over from the latter, who himself was the son of the owner of Phildar. Twenty-seven-year-old Antoine Arnault is named director to LVMH, the CEO of which is his father, Bernard, himself the son of the owner of Ferinel, a company with 1,000 employees. Antoine joins his sister Delphine, who joined the board in 2004.

In the United States, where business and politics are virtually united, "George Bush is the son of a president, the grandson of a senator, and the sprig of America's business aristocracy," writes the *Economist*.

> John Kerry, thanks to a rich wife, is the richest man in a Senate full of plutocrats. He is also a Boston Brahmin, educated at St. Paul's, a posh private school, and Yale— where, like the Bushes, he belonged to the ultra-select Skull and Bones society.
>
> Mr. Kerry's predecessor as the Democrats' presidential nominee, Al Gore, was the son of a senator. Mr. Gore, too, was educated at a posh private school, St. Albans, and then at Harvard. And Mr. Kerry's main challenger from the left of his party? Howard Brush Dean was the product of the same blue-blooded world of private schools and unchanging middle names as Mr. Bush. . . . Mr. Dean grew up in the Hamptons and on New York's Park Avenue. . . .
>
> Everywhere you look in modern America—in the Hollywood hills or the canyons of Wall Street, in the Nashville recording studios or the clapboard houses of Cambridge, Massachusetts—you see elites mastering the art of perpetuating themselves. America is increasingly looking like imperial Britain, with dynastic ties proliferating, social circles interlocking, mechanisms of social exclusion strengthening and a gap widening between the people who make the decisions and shape the culture and the vast majority of ordinary working stiffs.

The hyper-rich think of themselves as a new aristocracy. More than any academic study, anecdotes tell about the caste's obliviousness: when, for example, Mr. Pinault invited his acquaintance to admire the installation of his art collection, he chose to seat himself at the table of honor between "Her Majesty the former Empress of Iran Farah Diba and Her Grace the Duchess of Marlborough."

One of the most effective means to bolt the château doors is to make university studies, through which brilliant individuals may ordinarily accede to command positions, very onerous. Thus, the best universities or schools require tuition fees that are out of reach for the poor and less accessible all the time for the middle class. At Harvard University, students' median family income is $150,000. In Japan, people deplore "the present elitist orientation in education." Wealth today derives from hereditary status, just as was the case under the *ancien régime* before the French Revolution.

Like Sad Maniacs

A simple question is anything but anecdotal (and we'll see why in the next chapter): How do the plutocrats spend their money? This story recounted in *Forbes* gives you an idea: "Limited Brands billionaire Leslie Wexner kicked off the yacht wars in 1997 when he launched the 316-foot *Limitless*, at the time 110 feet longer than any other boat. Since then a competitive sport has emerged in waterlines. To play, you need to spend up to $300 million, and perhaps buy more than one vessel (Russian magnate Roman Abramovich owns three). Rumour has it Larry Ellison ordered his *Rising Sun* be built a few feet longer than Paul Allen's *Octopus*." The *Octopus* in question—at 413 feet—is equipped with a basketball court, a heliport, a movie theater, and a submarine in the hold. The French hyper-rich settle for less: 105 feet for Lindsay Owen-Jones's *Magic Carpet II*, 197 feet for Vincent Bolloré's *Paloma*.

Here are a few things *Forbes* used to gauge its cost of living "extremely well": a Russian fur coat at Bloomingdale's ($160,000 in 2005); twelve Turnbull and Asser shirts ($3,480); a case of Dom Pérignon champagne at Sherry-Lehmann ($1,559); and a pair of James Purdey and Sons rifles ($167,000). Among the other ways to use one's spending money, the gazettes mention that one may squander $241,000 in a night at a striptease club, as did Savvis CEO Robert McCormick; install air-conditioning in one's race-horses' stalls, as did the Brunei magnate, Haji Hassanal Bolkiah Mu'izzaddin Waddaulah; dress oneself in made-to-order at $7,300 per suit; treat oneself to the most expensive car in the world, the Bentley 728, for $1,200,000, or get the fastest car, the Koenigsegg CCR at 244 mph, for $723,000; join the most select—consequently the most expensive—club in the country, which in China would be the Chang An Club in Beijing, annual dues $18,000; or frequent a serious gym, such as the Sudbury, Massachusetts, Bosse Sports and Health Club with annual dues of $50,000.

One would, of course, buy spacious digs. A well-off fellow like Joseph Jacobs, manager of a speculative fund, is looking to build a 30,000-square-foot house in Greenwich, Connecticut, that includes four kitchens. In Paris, Bernard Arnault bought a 21,500-square-foot townhouse from Betty Lagardère for €45 million. David de Rothschild lives in a house on Rue du Bac; Jérôme Seydoux occupies a whole building on the Rue de Grenelle. In fact, one would have several houses, or residences, in the great capitals as well as in quiet spots—like Silvio Berlusconi's property in Sardinia, 27,000 square feet on 1,260 acres; or Jean-Marie Fourtou's place in Morocco, nine bedrooms with baths, twelve servants, and a heated 2,100-square-foot pool on 32 acres.

The art collection signals good taste—and allows a full tax deduction.

In a more prosaic vein, a London banker describes how he will spend the £500,000 bonus he got at the end of 2005: "Our financier expects to buy some land and enlarge his secondary residence in Bedfordshire, buy a new Bentley and a diamond necklace for his wife, and pay the fees for the prestigious private boarding schools his children attend. This soccer fanatic has also acquired a reserved seat for ten years at the new Wembley stadium for the modest sum of £36,400 pounds. The family will make a £10,000 donation to the fight against breast cancer. Finally, this City professional dashed after best-of-the-best vintages to enrich his cellar." In London, "sports car concessionaires, high-end restaurateurs, and luxury stores are rubbing their hands. With the 'gents' infatuation with Botox and liposuction, cosmetic surgeries are doing good business."

The rich, like the yokels, go on vacation: in 2005, the fashionable destinations seemed to be Venice, Mustique Island, and Patagonia. One eminent personage gives a good idea of the order of magnitude of the budget required in the good spots: Jacques Chirac at the Royal Palm Hotel in Mauritius, €3,350 a day in 2000. Closer to the people are Dominique Strauss-Kahn, now the director of the International Monetary Fund, and his wife, Anne Sinclair: "In July 1999," their biographers relate, "they declined the invitation of [then] World Bank head James Wolfensohn, who invited them to spend a few days at his ranch in the United States. They preferred to go to Egypt with their children before slipping off alone together to Asia. They also frequently fly away on the weekend to Morocco where the TF1 [the first European television network] clan is wont to go and where Dominique also likes to relive his memories. In winter, the family skis at Meribel, and, the last few years, at the Arcs."

But the real hyper-rich have their own airplane—or the company's—for $1.5 to $59 million. A plane is very useful for living out momentous experiences, such as Thierry Breton, then CEO at France Télécom, using one for a round-trip to the United States to watch a rugby match. It would be very important to fit out the interior with precious wood or marble. The well-advised manager consults the business-airplanes catalogue the way others choose a bicycle or electric saw; we would advise him to choose the Falcon 900EX, so relatively modest in its appetite—a ton less fuel consumed every 1,000 miles than its competitors—and which its manufacturer calls the "green machine". Oh, to fly in one's own plane and feel like a pure environmentalist.

Airplanes begin to look a bit outmoded, though. Isn't it more upmarket to spend one's bundle in space? It costs $20 million to spend a week in the International Space Station, as did Dennis Tito in May 2001, Mark Shuttleworth in 2002, and Gregory Olsen in 2005. But soon one should be able to find cheaper flights, for example, the $100,000 suborbital getaway organized by Space Adventures or the commercial tourist flights proposed for the future by Virgin Galactic for $200,000. To tell the truth, I don't know exactly why, but space flight already has a rather vulgar aspect, too 'look-at-me'. I'd advise you to buy a cruise submarine instead, such as the Phoenix that U.S. Subs offers made-to-order: more than 98 feet long, close to 400 tons, with apartments, big portholes to see outside, and two weeks' autonomy—Captain Nemo had better watch out. The bill—$43 million. But you're worth it, right?

Money is no longer hidden: on the contrary, one must display it. And for that, there's nothing better than a good party. François Pinault invited 920 of his 'friends' to Venice for the inauguration of his private museum. They came in private planes, of course, to the point that Marco Polo Airport was glutted—it was necessary to re-route some of the 160 jets to other airports, whence helicopters whisked their passengers to the city of the Doges. Mr.

Pinault was delighted: he outperformed his comrade Bernard Arnault, who counted 650 guests only at his daughter Delphine's wedding, "big, French-style nuptials," where "princes, stars and the barons of finance" assembled.

And the children? They divert themselves like sad maniacs: between Neuilly and Paris's 16th arrondissement, *Paris-Match* relates,

> the girls are named Chloé or Olympia and wear Gucci. The boys drive a convertible pending receipt of their licence. They all go to the same posh high schools, but often end up in a Baccalaureate factory; go out to 'L'Étoile', the 'Cab'' , or the 'Planches' for the youngest; go on holiday at the other end of the world. . . . They immediately talk about money and she tells you what she thinks: Daphné doesn't like the poor very much. . . . As for a career, it has to be easy. Otherwise Daddy will find them a job. And if not Papa, it will be one of his friends, as this gang of little boys seated at a table at Scossa bragged: 'There will always be a job for us, even if you find that unfair.'"

Here's Paris Hilton, the heiress to an eponymous hotel chain, and a billionaire, of whom we learn from the gazettes that she "has but one job in life: shopping." "And it's not easy to spend several million dollars in under twenty seconds. Yves Saint Laurent and Calvin Klein are her tutors." We follow her adventures, duly chronicled by the Associated Press, from lover—Greek heir Paris Latsis—to lover—Greek heir Stavros Niarchos—before he changes again.

The oligarchs live separated from the plebs. They are unaware how the poor and workers live; they don't know, and don't want to know.

If the hyper-rich live apart, that retreat from the collective space is imitated by the wealthy classes that envy them. In the United States, they increasingly live in separated cities, constituted of groups of private residences that are progressively immuring themselves. More than 10 million people already live within the shelter of these walls; the phenomenon leads to the creation of veritable cities, like Weston, Florida, where "the collection of gated communities forms a private city of 50,000 residents." The houses, refuges against the exterior world, are ever more spacious: according to the National Association of Home Builders, the average size of a house built in the United States has increased by over half between 1970 and 2004, although family size decreased at the same time.

"That America lives in its bubble," relates journalist Corine Lesnes. "Its residents don't have anything to do in the cities any more and go there infrequently. They drive stone-faced in slow-motion on over-crowded highways, each one busy with his unilateral pursuit of happiness and security."

The phenomenon is being duplicated in Latin America: Brazilian *condominios fechadaos*, Argentine country clubs, and Colombian *conjuntos cerrados*. In South Africa, the rich live sheltered in houses surrounded by barbed wire with a surveillance camera in the entry, while guards pass regularly in the protected streets. In France, in Toulouse, in Lille, in the Parisian region, one sees the increase in *résidences fermées*, connected fortresses under electronic and video surveillance, where through their television anyone may perform surveillance of the parking lots, lobbies, hallways, and lawns. "Today, my fear is that security requirements will become absurd, that we will end up with watchtowers," worries one Bouygues Real Estate promoter of these residences.

CHAPTER THREE

A Blind Oligarchy

That a caste of oligarchs, a layer of the hyper-rich, exists is not in itself, when seen from Sirius, a problem. It was frequently observed in the past that possession of power went hand in hand with the appropriation of great wealth. History is, in part, the tale of the ascension and then inevitable fall of such groups.

However, we are not on Sirius but on planet Earth. And we are at a specific moment in history, the twenty-first century, which poses a radically new challenge for the human species: for the first time since the beginning of its expansion more than a million years ago, it is running up against the biospheric limits of its prodigious dynamism. To truly live at this time means we must collectively find the paths to reorient this energy in other directions. It's a magnificent—but difficult—challenge.

But this predatory and rapacious ruling class, wasting its material assets, misusing power, stands as an immovable obstacle in those paths. It bears no plan, is animated by no ideal, delivers no promise. The aristocracy of the Middle Ages was not an exploitative caste only; it dreamed of building a transcendent order, dreams to which Gothic cathedrals splendidly bear witness. The nineteenth-century bourgeoisie that Karl Marx described as a revolutionary class exploited the proletariat but also felt it was propagating progress and humanist ideals. The ruling classes of the Cold War were borne along by the will to defend democratic freedoms in the face of a totalitarian counterexample.

But today, after triumphing over Sovietism, capitalism doesn't know how to do anything but celebrate itself. All spheres of power and influence have been swallowed by capitalism's pseudo-realism that asserts that any alternative is impossible and that the only end to pursue in order to soften the inevitability of injustice is to eke out ever more wealth.

This would-be realism is not only ominous; it is blind. Blind to the explosive power of manifest injustice. And blind to the poisoning of the biosphere that the increase in material wealth produces, poisoning that means deterioration in the conditions for human life and the squandering of the chances of generations to come.

You likely don't know Thorstein Veblen. That's to be expected. What isn't to be expected is that many economists don't know him either.

Raymond Aron, who was an unexcitable person, compared Veblen's works to those of Alexis de Tocqueville and Carl Von Clausewitz. For Veblen's thought is an essential key to understanding our era. Yet Veblen remains absent from university programs in economic science.

The man was the son of peasants. His father moved from Norway to Wisconsin ten years before Thorstein's birth in 1857. Norwegian was spoken in the home. Thorstein Veblen learned English as an adolescent and was a brilliant student, obtaining a doctorate in 1884 from Yale. Having scant inclination for the bowing and scraping necessary to assure himself a bourgeois position, he returned to the paternal farm for six years before resuming his studies at Cornell in 1891, and then immediately obtaining a teaching position at the University of Chicago. He lived a retired, if rather eccentric, existence, busy with rich intellectual labour. His first book, *Theory of the Leisure Class*, published in 1899, gave him an immediate and sustained notoriety from its first appearance. That was no doubt due to the context of the time: the beginning of the twentieth century was the apogee of what historians called "untamed capitalism" in the United States (as it was in Europe also, but in another form).

Then Veblen was forgotten. Incomes narrowed a great deal over the course of the twentieth century, which made the interest in his analysis less immediate. But the return of great inequality and the present situation of heightened capitalism drunk on itself restores to the Chicago economist all his original incisive freshness.

For Veblen, the economy is dominated by a principle: "the propensity for emulation—for invidious comparison—is of ancient growth and is a pervading trait of human nature." "With the exception of the instinct for self-preservation," he notes, "the propensity for emulation is probably the strongest and most alert and persistent of the economic motives proper." The idea had been suggested by the founder of classical economics, Adam Smith. In his *Theory of Moral Sentiments*, he noted that "the love of distinction, so natural to man . . . rouses and keeps in continual motion the industry of mankind." But Smith never really delved into this principle that Veblen, on the contrary, systematized.

According to Veblen, human societies left a natural and peaceful state for one of brutal rapacity in which struggle is the principle of existence. The resulting differentiation between a leisure class and a working class has held even as society evolved toward less violent phases. But the possession of wealth has remained as the means of differentiation, its essential objective being not to answer a material need but to assure a 'provocative distinction'; in other words, to exhibit the signs of superior status.

Certainly, part of the production of goods responds to 'useful purposes' and satisfies concrete needs of existence. But the level of production necessary to these useful ends is rather easily reached. And, starting from that level, the extra production is generated by the desire to display one's wealth so as to distinguish oneself from everyone else, which feeds conspicuous consumption and generalized waste.

There's No Need to Increase Production

Veblen's first original insight is to reverse the founding axiom of classical economics. Classical economics reasons from a universe of constraints in which men have limited resources to meet unlimited need. Under that scenario, the economic question is how to increase production to increase the supply of goods and try to satisfy needs. Veblen, on the contrary, observed that needs are not infinite. Above a certain level, it's the social contest that stimulates them. In the same way, he did not consider production to be scarce but postulated that it is adequate.

This approach constitutes a radical departure from the economic discourse that makes up the dominant ideology. From that point of view, capitalism and Marxism are strictly equivalent: they both postulate that production is inadequate. Veblen turns the analysis upside down: production is adequate; the question posed by the economy bears on the reasons and rules of consumption.

One of Veblen's sources of information was the ethnography of the peoples of the Americas and the Pacific. Those cultures were often still thriving in the nineteenth century. Thus, in Chicago Veblen met Franz Boas, an ethnographer who had studied the Kwakiutl Indians of the Pacific Northwest. The Kwakiutl, who enjoyed great prosperity from fishing and fur trapping, practiced the 'potlatch': during long feasts, they indulged in a sort of competition of gifts, each gift that one clan gave another calling for another still more beautiful present in return, which the first clan would reciprocate, going one step further in a cycle of munificence that ended in a debauchery of possessions. Boas's observation was not unique. The potlatch has been described in different forms in numerous societies, to the point that French sociologist Marcel Mauss presented it in his *Essay on the Gift* (1923) as a "general system of economy and law".

Let's remember the lesson of this ethnographic tradition: the natural regime of societies is not discomfort; they may also experience an abundance that allows a considerable surplus to be wasted. Veblen was the first to understand the importance of that observation, and he built his thesis on it.

The Upper Class Defines the Lifestyle of Its Era

Veblen reasoned that the principle of conspicuous consumption governs society. Society has diversified itself into several strata, each of which behaves according to the same principle of distinction, that is, by seeking to imitate the layer above. "Each class envies and emulates the class next above it in social scale, while it rarely compares itself with those below or those that are considerably in advance," Veblen writes. "In other words, our standard of decency in expenditure, as in other ends of emulation, is set by the usage of those next above us in reputability; until, in this way, especially in any community where class distinctions are somewhat vague, all canons of reputability and decency, and all standards of consumption, are traced back by insensible gradations to the usages and habits of the highest social and pecuniary class—the wealthy leisure class. It is for this class to determine, in general outline, what scheme of life the community shall accept as decent or honorific."

Veblen's language is a little convoluted yet nonetheless clear. Let us simply say that Veblen compares the capitalist society he knows—"where class distinctions are somewhat vague"—to aristocratic societies, for example, the English or French monarchies of the eighteenth century.

Imitation leads to a torrent of waste, the source of which is situated at the top of the human mountain. "The leisure class," the economist continues, stands at the head of the social structure in point of reputability; and its manner of life and its standards of worth therefore afford the norm of reputability for the community. The observance of these standards, in some degree of approximation, becomes incumbent on all classes lower in the scale. In modern civilized societies the lines of demarcation between social classes have grown vague and transient, and whenever this happens the norm of reputability imposed by the upper classes extends its coercive influence with but slight hindrance down through the social structure to the lowest strata. The result is that the members of each stratum accept as their ideal of decency the scheme of life in vogue in the next higher stratum and bend their energies to live up to that ideal.

Insatiable Competition

Let's summarize. The central drive of social life, Veblen says, is ostentatious rivalry that aims to exhibit prosperity superior to one's peers. Society's division into numerous strata excites an overall or general competition.

The race for distinction pushes society to produce much more than what 'useful purposes' would require: "As increased industrial efficiency makes it possible to procure the means of livelihood with less labour, the energies of the industrious members of the community are bent to the compassing of a higher result in conspicuous expenditure, rather than slackened to a more comfortable pace. The strain is not lightened as industrial efficiency increases and makes a lighter strain possible, but the increment of output is turned to use to meet this want, which is indefinitely expansible, after the manner commonly imputed in economic theory to higher or spiritual wants." In fact, one never stops: think about our billionaires. What to buy when everyone has his plane decorated with precious wood and marble? An art collection? A rocket? A submarine? And then? A holiday on the moon? Something else, always, since satiety does not exist in sumptuary competition.

Finally, the leisure class, at the summit, cuts itself off from society. "To the individual of high breeding it is only the more honorific esteem accorded by the cultivated sense of the members of his own class that is of material consequence. Since the wealthy leisure class has grown so large, or the contact of the leisure class individual with members of his own class has grown so wide, as to constitute a human environment sufficient for the honorific purpose, there arises a tendency to exclude the baser elements of the population from the scheme even as spectators whose applause or mortification should be sought."

Veblen's theory seems so clear that there's hardly any need to comment on it. Let's observe our oligarchs. And let's look at how the SUVs, the trips to Hong Kong or to Prague, the extra-flat TV screens, digital cameras, television telephones, highly technical coffee makers, and incommensurable piling up of the objects that compose the decor of our opulent societies cascades down in stages to the most modest ranks of society as their discovery by the hyper-rich recedes in ever more frenetic times. But the filters of each person's possibilities as one descends the ladder of wealth cruelly limit the flood of fruits from the horn of abundance. They leave unsatisfied the inextinguishable desire that the oligarchs' razzle-dazzle squandering stimulates.

The Invisible Border of the New *Nomenklatura*

At this point, I think it's time to summarize what we know about the oligarchic societies of globalized humanity at the beginning of the twenty-first century.

At the apex, there is a caste of the hyper-rich, a group consisting of several tens of thousands of persons or families. They bathe in a larger milieu that one could call the capitalist version of the Soviet *nomenklatura*: the upper class, less rich than the hyper-rich, although very opulent, obeys the latter, or at least respects them. Along with the hyper-rich, the *nomenklatura* holds the levers of global society's political and economic power.

Two representatives of the French branch of the oligarchy describe it this way. For Alain Minc, it's the totality of "politicians on the ground, the executive directors of business, men of culture, teachers of higher learning, scientific researchers, entry-level reporters, provincial magistrates, Category A bureaucrats, those with high school diplomas 'plus 5, 7, or 9 years additional schooling,' of whom only a few succeed in penetrating the 'Sanhedrin' of the super-elite, but who all live with the same mental reflexes and the same intellectual code."

For Jean Peyrelevade, modern capitalism is organized like a gigantic corporation. At the base, 300 million owners (out of 6 billion humans, or 5 percent of the world's population) control the quasi-totality of global market capitalization. These are "ordinary citizens of rich countries, assured of their political as well as social legitimacy," he notes, and they confide half of their financial assets to some tens of thousands of managers whose sole objective is to enrich their own positions.

Minc and Peyrelevade push the borders further down than they actually go—"those with high school diplomas 'plus 5, 7, or 9 years additional schooling,' entry-level reporters, ordinary citizens"—in order to enlarge the caste, which makes it less unbearable, but the categorization, the invisible and bolted border, is evoked.

The capitalist *nomenklatura* adopts the sumptuary canons of the hyper-rich and diffuses them to the middle classes, which reproduce them to the extent of their means and are themselves imitated by the poor classes.

The hyper-rich and the *nomenklatura* constitute the oligarchy. These individuals indulge in a rough internal competition, an exhausting race for power and ostentation. To stay in the race, and neither falter nor wane, they always have to have more. They organize a growing withdrawal from society's collective wealth. Solidly controlling the levers of power, they close off the middle class, the progeny of which no longer succeed in integrating themselves within their own caste except with difficulty.

This middle class constitutes an ever-softer underbelly of society, while it was once social capitalism's centre of gravity during its short Golden Age centred on the 1960s. Still too attracted to the oligarchy's flames to bask or exhaust itself at its own level in the race for conspicuous consumption, it is beginning to understand that its dream of social ascension is dissolving. It is even seeing the up-to-now closed lower border between it and the world of workers and lower-level employees becoming more permeable.

And, in the same way, those workers and low-level employees are losing any hope of penetrating the middle class. Quite the contrary, the increasing precariousness of employment, the weakening the oligarchy desired of the frameworks for collective solidarity, and the increased cost of education allows them to glimpse a descent toward those from whom they thought themselves separated—the mass of the poor—who, in rich countries, struggle in the discomfort of a daily life composed of noodles, cheap canned food, and unpaid bills. Crouching in this gnawing mediocrity lingers the threat of slipping into the degradation of the street, alcoholism, and anonymous death in the small hours of a freezing morning.

The United States' Oligarchy at the Peak of Sumptuary Competition

At this point, two remarks are necessary.

First of all, if Veblen is as important as I, along with Raymond Aron, assert, how is it that people don't talk about him more? In fact, he's beginning to be rediscovered, and some economists are doing more than re-reading him; they're applying his theory to modern econometric methods. Thus, it has been recently shown, for example, that the level of English workers' satisfaction correlates with the degree to which their peers' salary is lower than their own. And that households with a lower income than their reference group save less than those whose income is higher in order to be able to consume more and keep up with the level of the second group.

In November 2005, the Royal Economic Society in Britain published another interesting study. Samuel Bowles and Yongjin Park showed, by using the Veblenian mechanism, that the time spent working increases in proportion to the degree of social inequality. In fact, in a given society, individuals collectively adapt their work time to the income desired. Now, the researchers observe that the income desired is a function of the distance that separates the individuals of one income group from the higher reference group. The greater that distance, that is, the greater the inequality, the more individuals try to work to increase their income. And, in fact, the length of time worked annually decreases from the most unequal countries (the United States) to the least (the Scandinavian countries).

Bowles and Park come to a logical conclusion from their demonstration. A policy that would tax the groups that serve as a reference for consumption "would be doubly attractive: it would increase the well-being of the least well-off by limiting Veblen's cascade effect and would supply funds for useful social projects."

A second remark is that we can bring Veblen up-to-date with the conditions of our era by widening his argument to the planet, given the globalization of cultural models. In each country, social groups try to copy the lifestyle of the local oligarchy, but the local oligarchy takes the oligarchies of the opulent countries as its model, and particularly the richest of those, the United States. Meanwhile, the countries themselves, as countries, are subject to Veblenian imitation. Now, Western societies, in spite of the inequality that characterizes them more and more, are nonetheless far richer collectively than the countries of the South. The countries of the South are in a catch-up race that is all the more frenetic as the gap gets wider.

Growth Is Not the Solution

Now let's resume the course of our discussion. Unbridled consumption driven by the oligarchy wounds justice by virtue of its unequal distribution.

Sure. But so what?

We've learned with Veblen that ostentation and imitation determine the economic game. We had observed in the first chapter that our civilization's level of material consumption is enormous and exerts excessive pressure on the biosphere.

Why then are the present characteristics of the global ruling class the essential factor in the environmental crisis?

Because this class opposes the radical changes that we would have to conduct to prevent the aggravation of the situation.

How?

Indirectly, by the status of its consumption: its model drags general consumption up by impelling others to imitate it. Directly, by control of economic and political power that allows it to maintain this inequality.

To escape any re-evaluation, the oligarchy keeps repeating the dominant ideology according to which the solution to the social crisis is production growth. That is supposedly the sole means of fighting poverty and unemployment. Growth would allow the overall level of wealth to rise and consequently improve the lot of the poor without—and this part is never spelled out—any need to modify the distribution of wealth.

This mechanism has become jammed up. According to economist Thomas Piketty, "The observation in the 1980s that inequality had since the 1970s begun to increase in Western countries again delivered a fatal blow to the idea of a curve inexorably linking development and inequality." Growth, moreover, does not create an adequate number of jobs, even in China, where, in spite of an extraordinary expansion in GNP, only 10 million new jobs appear every year while 20 million people join the job market. "Market theory," explains Juan Somavia, director general of the UN's International Labour Organization, "requires that growth create wealth, which is redistributed through job creation, which feeds consumption, which generates new investment and consequently the production cycle. But from the moment the link between growth and employment is broken, this virtuous circle no longer operates as it's supposed to."

Moreover, and this crucial point is always forgotten by growth zealots, growth has an enormous and harmful effect on the environment, which today we know is in a state of extreme fragility. I must insist on this point. Is this assertion that growth degrades the environment established? Is there not a 'decoupling' of growth and environmental degradation? The term 'decoupling' designates a situation in which the economy grows without increasing environmental pressure.

The answer to that question was supplied by economists from the Organization for Economic Cooperation and Development (OECD), an agency that brings together Western governments, Japan and Korea. In its *Environmental Perspectives* presented in May 2001, the OECD observed that economic growth in developed countries does not improve the ecological situation. "Environmental degradation has generally advanced at a slightly lesser pace than that of economic growth," the experts summarized; "the pressures [that] consumption exerts on the environment have intensified during the second half of the twentieth century and during the next twenty years, they should continue to increase."

The environment in the OECD countries has been cleaned up in only a few respects: atmospheric lead emissions, chlorofluorocarbons (CFCs—substances that destroy the ozone layer), and atmospheric fuels such as nitrogen oxide and carbon monoxide have been significantly reduced. Water consumption is stabilizing. Forested acreage is increasing slightly—although its biodiversity is still declining because of the massive fragmentation that roads introduce. For the remainder, the situation is worsening: overfishing, pollution of subterranean water, greenhouse gas emissions, production of household waste, the spread of chemicals, fine particulate atmospheric pollution, soil erosion and radioactive waste production have all been increasing constantly since 1980.

How is that possible? Because the "volume impacts of the growth in total production and consumption have more than compensated for the efficiency gains per unit produced." If, for example, technological improvement decreases each car's pollution, that reduction is not adequate to compensate for the overall increase in the number of cars. Even if developed countries have more or less improved their energy intensity (the relationship of energy consumption per GNP unit) and their materials intensity (the relationship of materials consumption per GNP unit) after twenty years, that progress is counterbalanced by the overall increase in GNP. In this way, "the overall consumption of natural resources in OECD regions has constantly increased." In several areas of the environment, moreover, there is not even any relative progress, because wealth pushes the growth in net consumption: roads multiply, air-conditioning spreads, electronic gadgetry diversifies, travel is easier, and so on.

Emergency: Reduce Consumption by the Rich

So, then, does growth reduce inequality? No, as economists have recorded for the last decade.

Does growth reduce poverty? With the present social structure, only when growth reaches levels that are unsustainable over the long term, as in China, where even that progress is reaching its limits.

Does growth improve the ecological situation? No, it aggravates it.

Every rational being should either demonstrate that these three conclusions are wrong or be wary of growth. There are no serious arguments against these three conclusions—about which several international agencies and many observers agree in restrained tones. And yet not one accredited economist, political official, or dominant media outlet criticizes growth, which has become the great taboo, the blind spot of contemporary thought.

Why? Because the pursuit of *material growth* is the oligarchy's only means of getting societies to accept extreme inequalities without questioning them. In effect, growth creates a surplus of apparent wealth that allows the system to be lubricated without modifying its structure.

What is the solution to escaping from the deadly trap in which the 'leisure class', to apply Veblen's term, has ensnared us? Stopping material growth. I emphasize the words 'material growth'—defined as the continual increase in goods produced by the appropriation and degradation of biospheric resources.

Unlike growth worshipers who treat you like an obstructionist as soon as you question their dogma rather than discuss it with you, I have no position in principle with respect to growth. If someone proves growth, as we know it, does not damage the environment any further, it would be acceptable. It's not condemnable in itself if one considers it as the execution of activity and inventiveness of an ever more numerous humanity. What creates the danger is that under present conditions, growth manifests itself as an increase in material production that harms the environment. If growth were immaterial, that is, if it increased wealth without consuming more natural resources, the problem would be altogether different. Consequently, the question is not how to achieve 'zero growth', but how to move toward 'material decline'. If humanity takes the planet's ecology seriously, it must put a ceiling on its overall material consumption and, if possible, decrease it.

How? There can be no question of decreasing the material consumption of the world's poorest, that is, the majority of the inhabitants of the countries of the South and some of the residents of rich countries. On the contrary, their consumption must be increased out of concern for justice.

Good. Then who today consumes the most material products? The hyper-rich? Not only they do. Individually, certainly, they waste outrageously, but collectively they don't weigh all that heavily. The oligarchy? Yes, that begins to create a critical mass. But that's still not enough. Together, North America, Europe, and Japan include a billion inhabitants, or less than 20 percent of the global population. And they consume about 80 percent of global wealth. Consequently, this billion people must reduce their material consumption. Among that billion, not the poor, but also not only the worst of the upper layer. Let's say 500 million people, and let's call them the global middle class. There's a pretty strong chance that you—like me—belong to this group of people who could usefully reduce their material consumption, their energy expenditures, their car and air travel.

But would we limit our waste and try to change our own lifestyle while the Fat Cats, up there, continue to luxuriate in their air-conditioned SUVs and their villas with swimming pools? No. The only way you and I will agree to consume less material and less energy is if the material consumption—and consequently the income—of the oligarchy is severely reduced. For itself, for reasons of equity, and still more, following on the lesson of that eccentric rascal Veblen, to change the cultural standards of conspicuous consumption. Since the leisure class establishes society's consumption model, if its level is reduced, the general level of consumption will decrease. We will consume less; the planet will be better off; and we'll be less frustrated by what we don't have.

The path is clear. But will the hyper-rich, the *nomenklatura,* go along with it?

5 | DEMOCRACY IN DANGER

Here's a little story that belongs to the specific and exact category of 'not believing my own eyes'.

In 2001, immediately after the September 11 attacks in New York, I fell upon a piece of intelligence so surprising I felt it necessary to study it with extra attention. After a thorough investigation, it was confirmed that the United States government was seriously considering using little nuclear bombs in potential conflicts, breaking with the 1978 doctrine prescribing no use of nuclear weapons against enemies that did not have any of their own. The investigation revealed that a bomb of this type had been perfected, the B61-11.

You can be sure that on a topic like this, I had verified all available information twice rather than once. What's interesting is that, once it was ready, the article was blocked for several weeks before it was published. My colleagues in the International Service rejected it because they could not bring themselves to accept that the information was correct in spite of the accumulated proofs. I had to do battle and refer to the editor-in-chief at the time to get the article published—it had a useful impact, incidentally, but that's another story.

Thus, it happens, and more frequently than people think, that true things are not accepted, or only with great difficulty, by the collective awareness. What could we have a problem believing today? Here's one: the global oligarchy wants to get rid of democracy and the civil rights and public liberties that constitute its substance.

The assertion is brutal. Let me formulate it another way: in the face of the turbulence engendered by the global environmental and social crises, and in order to preserve its own privileges, the oligarchy chooses to weaken the spirit and the forms of democracy, that is to say, free discussion of collective choices; respect for the law and its representatives; protections of individual liberties vis-à-vis the encroachments of the state; and other constituted entities.

As far as Western countries are concerned, when we think about dictatorship, Mussolini, Hitler, and Stalin come to mind. The comparison is misleading. What is happening in front of our eyes cannot be compared to those three regimes, for the times have changed, as well as the forms of political life and the techniques of social control. Rather than violent dictatorships, the oligarchy prefers the progressive bastardization of democracy.

Someone formulated this idea very well more than a century ago:

> The kind of oppression that threatens democratic peoples does not in any way resemble what preceded it. . . . I want to imagine what aspect despotism could take on in the world: I see an innumerable crowd of men, similar to one another and equal, who gyrate unceasingly in order to obtain small and vulgar pleasures for themselves with which they fill their souls. Each one of them, isolated at some remove from the others, is like a stranger to the destiny of all the others: his children and his personal friends constitute the entire human species for him: as for the remainder of his fellow citizens, he is right next to them, but he doesn't see them; he touches them and doesn't feel them; he exists only within and for himself, and, although he still has a family, one may at the least say he no longer has a country. Above all

these men rises an immense tutelary power that alone assures their enjoyment and watches over their fate. It is absolute, elaborate, regular, calculating, and mild. It would be like paternal power, if—like it—its goal was to prepare men for virile maturity; but, on the contrary, it seeks only to limit them irrevocably to childhood; it likes its citizens to be happy, as long as they dream of nothing other than being happy.

This eloquent author is a man of—if one is to believe Raymond Aron—the same quality as Veblen: the quote is from Alexis de Tocqueville.

The Terrorism Alibi

The anti-democratic drift started in the 1990s with the triumph of a capitalism liberated from the pressure of its enemy, Sovietism. The dysfunction of the U.S. electoral machinery in 2000, which brought the candidate who had less votes that his opponent to power, was its visible emergence for those who had not been alerted to the implementation of the Echelon system by the United States in 1996, which allowed it to listen to its allies' communications. But the offensive against civil liberties enjoyed an extraordinary boon with the September 11, 2001, attacks in New York and Washington. Those events disinhibited—if that were necessary—the team created by President George W. Bush—all, moreover, men and women involved as executives or members of the boards of directors of numerous big companies, often in the defence sector.

The first episode was the authorization of the 500-plus-page Patriot Act less than fifteen days after the attacks—its passage into law accelerated in the name of the fight against terrorism. The text spread procedures previously reserved for foreign spies to all U.S. citizens: recording of telephone conversations, e-mail surveillance, possible searches without a warrant, and searches of medical, library, bank and travel agency records, among other private documents. The law also provided for the reduction of judicial or Congressional oversight of these investigations. It was re-authorized, practically without modification, in March 2006.

It took almost five years for the press to discover that the National Security Agency (NSA) was monitoring U.S. citizens' foreign telephone conversations without authorization from the special court created for that purpose. At the same time, people learned that the NSA was also examining e-mails transiting through the three biggest telecommunications companies, AT&T, Verizon, and BellSouth—Qwest alone having refused to collaborate. The NSA, which is part of the Defense Department, has a budget perhaps ten times the size of that of the Central Intelligence Agency (CIA) and concentrates perhaps the most important computing power in the world at Fort Meade, Maryland.

The U.S. administration's curiosity also extends to banking transactions, through a clandestine surveillance program, the so-called Terrorist Finance Tracking Program. First intended to be temporary, it has become permanent. The United States' government is even concerning itself with air travel: a piece of legislation adopted in 2001 requires that companies making flights with a U.S. destination or departure or transiting U.S. territory must supply the customs authorities with access to the data in their reservation systems, including about fifty discrete pieces of information concerning travellers' identity, itinerary, residence, health, dietary preferences, and so on. With respect to the European Union, the Commission and the Council of

Ministers acceded to the U.S. requirement to bow to this rule, trying to circumvent the European Parliament's opposition. In any case, the system leads the U.S. authorities to prohibit several tens of thousands of people, inscribed on lists of individuals deemed dangerous, from flying. Such glaringly obvious terrorists as Ted Kennedy, Democratic senator from Massachusetts, James Moore, author of a book about Bush advisor Karl Rove, and Robert Johnson, a Democratic candidate opposing the war in Iraq, have, in this way, been prevented from flying.

Let's Celebrate the 'Security Agency Worker'

The United States has set up internment camps abroad—one in Guantánamo, Cuba, the other at Bagram, close to Kabul in Afghanistan—in order to evade the Geneva Conventions on the treatment of war prisoners. Men arrested during the U.S. invasion of Afghanistan in 2001–02 are imprisoned in Guantánamo without any legal protection. It happened that some of the prisoners succeeded in committing suicide there; Guantánamo Base commandant Harry Harris opined at the time that the suicides were not "an act of desperation, but an act of asymmetrical warfare waged against the United States."

In the eyes of common opinion, the United States remains the premier democracy in the world. So, this 'democracy' reinstated the use of torture. In 2002, President Bush signed a secret decree authorizing the CIA to establish hidden detention centres outside the United States and to interrogate prisoners harshly at these centres, his top legal advisor Alberto Gonzales having indicated to him that the Geneva Convention "does not apply to the conflict with al-Qaeda." Since then, as has been well documented, the world's premier power has "disappeared detainees in a network of secret prisons by kidnapping and sending people for interrogation to countries where torture is practiced such as Egypt, Syria, or Morocco," summarized Larry Cox, Amnesty International's director for the United States.

The term that designates torture in this new world is 'enhanced interrogation technique'. I will refrain from presenting the reader with examples of these 'enhanced techniques'. They leave nothing to envy in the practices of the Gestapo's 'technicians'.

The abuse inflicted on detainees at the Abu Ghraib prison in Baghdad, revealed in 2004, is nothing but the tip of the iceberg of the 'war against terror'. In 2006, close to 14,500 'suspects' were detained in these dungeons located outside the United States. Several European countries assisted the CIA in the transfer of prisoners to the torture centres established in different places around the world, authorizing the U.S. agency's planes to land at their airports, closing their eyes to the kidnapping of 'suspects' on their territory, even—but the fact has not been definitively established for Poland and Romania—harbouring such prisons.

Secretary of State Condoleezza Rice declares that "it is our duty to bring countries that do not respect their human rights commitments into line." In February 2006, Russia adopted an antiterrorism law that authorizes the security forces to "freely penetrate" individuals' homes, to wiretap telephone conversations, to intercept regular mail and e-mail, and to limit, if necessary, individuals' movement. The same law also restricts the freedom to demonstrate and journalists' freedom. Anti-terrorist commissions directed by the FSB (the KGB's new name) are implemented alongside existing governmental structures. On December 20 of each year, the population is invited to celebrate 'the day of the security agency worker'.

In Germany, the *Länder* (regional states) have created data files on several million people that include, for example, their ethnicity and religion.

In Great Britain at the beginning of 2006, Amnesty International characterized the government's human rights record as "damning". Foreigners detained for several years without charge, suspects put under residential surveillance without recourse to the courts, and suspects deported to countries that use torture are among the behaviours the organization deplored. Shortly before, Prime Minister Blair wanted to extend custody without charges from fourteen to forty-eight days, which Parliament rejected. Belgium introduced the notion of 'specific research methods' by the police into a new anti-terrorist law. The European Union adopted a directive strengthening legislation concerning the preservation of telephone and other electronic records.

In France, in December 2005, Parliament adopted its eighth anti-terrorist law. Like the preceding ones, it strengthens police powers. The text extends custody without charge to six days, lifts administrative and legal constraints against certain monitoring and surveillance procedures, extends the possibility of video surveillance by private operators, facilitates identity controls, obliges transportation companies to communicate passenger data, makes possible the systematic photography of vehicle occupants on the roads, allows the police services to consult telecommunications and Internet providers' data banks without any judiciary supervision, and so on and so forth. "The proposed provisions all, without exception, constitute new attacks or restrictions on fundamental freedoms," deems the Magistrates' Union.

It matters that Westerners are afraid—the others, as we know, have hardly enjoyed the privilege of tasting democracy. The Bush administration repeats ad nauseam that we must make 'war on terror'. "We are a nation at war," proclaims the *National Security Strategy* the White House published in 2006. This war has a virtue: it justifies the changes that have been made to human rights. Five years of overkill seem to have been effective with U.S. public opinion. Type the word 'terrorism', for example, into Google and the number of occurrences found on a day in 2006 was 337 *million*. The word 'democracy' brings up fewer occurrences at 289 million. At that time, terrorism beat democracy as an Internet user concern. Bravo, President Bush!

As the scholar Medhi Belhaj Kacem wrote, "This so-perfect democracy itself manufactures its inconceivable enemy, terrorism: far from threatening [democracy], [terrorism] is the ultimate proof of its perpetual maintenance: since [democracy] will never again have to be judged for its results, but for its enemies." Let's call torture 'enhanced interrogation techniques', and call the regime promoted by President Bush and his European friends 'democracy', and all will be well: freedom will prosper.

A Policy for the Poor: Prison

Alongside the bogeyman of terrorism, it's useful to wave another straw man: crime and security.

When not tackled politically or by the collective conscience, social inequality increases frustration and the desperate need to find a way out. Hence the pressure of 'crime' in rich countries and the pressure of migration from the South toward the North. To contain the effects of causes that they poorly understand, the lower and middle classes demand more 'security' and accept the initially imperceptible reduction in the level of public freedoms.

In the arsenal of the war against the poor, the first weapon is prison. In the United States, the number of prisoners reached 2.2 million in 2005—it was 500,000 in 1980. And a new study by the Pew Center on the States found that between 2007 and 2011 that number will grow by another 200,000, and that currently more than one out of every 100 adults is behind bars in the United States. It's the highest level in the whole world. You'd have to go look in the gulags of Stalin's Russia or Mao Ze Dong's China to find a higher number. That represents 738 prisoners per 100,000 inhabitants, seven times more, proportionally, than in France, which itself confines people with enthusiasm. One sign indicates the misery and suffering this situation involves: in 2005, Congress had to establish a commission for the elimination of rape in prison.

Moreover, the quality of "medical and psychiatric care in prisons goes from mediocre to terrible," writes Human Rights Watch in its annual human rights report.

Prison does not strike the entire population equally: according to the statistics of the U.S. Bureau of Justice, 11.9 percent of African-American men between the ages of 25 and 29 were in prison, versus 3.9 percent of Hispanic men and 1.7 percent of white men in the same age group. The U.S. situation influences, let us note, other statistics: when economists applaud the supposedly low unemployment rate in the United States, they omit to mention that you would have to raise that number by at least 1 percent to take into account the fact that many people in prison, if they were free, would be unemployed.

In France, the incarceration rate has continued to increase during the last thirty years to reach a historic record of 98 per 100,000 inhabitants. The number of prisoners went from 29,500 in 1971 to 59,000 in 2005 (the reduction that began in 1996 was interrupted in 2002). That's less than in Germany (78,600 prisoners in 2006) or in the United Kingdom (79,000).

French laws that increasingly restrict the legal freedoms and guarantees of the citizen in the face of the government arrive in rapid succession and come on top of the laws on terrorism:

the November 15, 2001, law of 'everyday security'; the March 18, 2003, law 'on domestic security'; the March 9, 2004, Perben 2 law ('adapting the justice system to developments in criminality'); the June 2006 law 'on crime prevention'. The texts broaden the grounds for genetic data filing, which was originally reserved for sexual crimes, introduce the notion of the 'organized gang' to justify exceptional procedures, lift limitations on vehicle searches by the police, increase the investigatory powers of the judicial police to the detriment of the rights of defence, transform the mayor into the coordinator of crime prevention, favour the creation of municipal data files on those receiving social assistance payments, provide a tax deduction for the installation of surveillance cameras, create closed education centres for minors under sixteen, provide for the placement of children as young as ten years old in special education establishments, and make occupying transportation infrastructures a crime.

Criminalizing Political Protest

Democracy is also daily betrayed by the government's arrangements with the legal system. In the domains of labour and immigration law, I understand that the codes are often disregarded. But being relatively unfamiliar with those domains, I won't say anything about them. On the other hand, with respect to environmental laws, it's clear that when the oligarchy has decided on something, it disdains the rules that discomfit it. In France, for example, with respect to nuclear matters, the government refused to hold departmental referenda about the radioactive waste in Haute-Marne and Meuse, in spite of more than 50,000 signatures, that is, over 20 percent of the citizens registered to vote (the 2003 law requires 10 percent); appealed to 'defence secrets' to prevent a discussion about the effect of a plane crash on the new kind of nuclear reactor, the so-called EPR; hid from the deputies debating the matter an opinion containing reservations expressed by the administration charged with examining its safety; organized a public debate on the construction of the so-called ITER fusion reactor when the decision had already been made; and so on. With respect to genetically modified organisms (GMOs), the government rejected the organization of a departmental referendum demanded by the Gers General Council; it has then gone on to systematically attack the dozens of municipal bylaws the communes are passing to prevent the cultivation of transgenic plants they don't want, hide the presence of those crops (although the European directive requires public registration), prevent communication of the toxicity evaluation files for GMOs to prevent a resurvey of the possible health problems they reveal, and so on.

It is interesting to see how the new laws allow the government to act against anti-establishment types just as much as against terrorists. In January 2006, for example, three people who could be considered 'anti-GMO reapers' were held in custody for several hours. They were interrogated in the framework of a legal investigation 'for participation in a criminal organization'. No specific charges were made against the people who were interrogated, and because of that their lawyer was not given access to the case file. Meanwhile, documents and computer hard drives were seized. Similarly, the spokesperson for the network Sortir du Nucléaire (Get Out of Nuclear Power) spent several hours in custody in May 2006 'under the control of the antiterrorist section' that was looking for the source of the EDF document showing that EPR is vulnerable to an aircraft crash. There again: search, computer seizure, no access to the file. Many 'anti-GMO reapers' are convicted for their refusal to be registered in the genetic information bank that was originally limited to sexual criminals.

Towards Total Surveillance

The 'neo-democrats' are in charge of social control techniques that the despots of the past could not have dreamed of. Thus, each one of us is classified numerous times, with the police and other administrations having ever more easy access to this data—without our knowledge, of course. Catalogues of genetic signatures are being developed: the United Kingdom leads the way for Europe with three million samples, or five percent of the population, versus 'only' 125,000 in France. Such an unfortunate accident: the British data bank contains many more samples from blacks than from whites.

Video surveillance cameras have sprung up in the last decade like mushrooms after rain. We find them in buses, businesses, residential quarters, stores, and streets. The United Kingdom is the video-surveillance-camera champion—it had more than four million such cameras in 2004. In 2006, the English police established an immense data bank that allows it to record vehicle movements, as computers are able to read licence plates day and night by way of cameras placed on the highways and in the cities. Every day, the movement of 35 million licence plates is recorded and held for two years. Police officials are ecstatic: it's "the greatest advance in crime detection technology since the introduction of DNA testing".

As this progress pushes on, a British Interior Ministry research service works on computer programmes capable of recognizing human faces that could be coupled with the cameras that monitor the streets and public places.

Private inventors create other systems. For example, the Mosquito. It's a housing and speaker that transmits powerful and unpleasant sounds on a specific frequency audible only to children and adolescents. With this, one can chase young people away from the places where they tend to gather. The inventor, Howard Stapleton, is preparing a hyper-powerful prototype, able to cover large areas forbidden to the public, such as switching yards and construction sites. Or streets during demonstrations?

Ideally, passers-by and vehicles should identify themselves to the monitoring services. So we see electronic labels being developed called radio frequency identification (RFID), radio frequency microchips or transponders that contain information about the object or the being that wears them. When it passes in front of a chip reader, that information is captured without the wearer's knowledge. These transponders have the information capacity of a 1985 microcomputer. In the most highly developed systems, the chip-reading apparatus can be located 100 yards away from the transponder wearer and still capture the data as he passes at top speed.

More than one billion RFID chips could be sold annually. Businesses are planning to use them in all the items they sell to ensure their product's traceability. An improvement in commercial efficiency? Undoubtedly. But one that contains certain risks. Let's imagine, for example, that these electronic labels are placed on books. Thus one could locate anyone who buys a book, such as this book, associating the environment, social inequalities, oligarchy, and democracy. The association Pièces et main-d'oeuvre imagines what a chip reader installed on the sidewalk could provide: "The Tex brand coat, size 42, number 987328765, purchased November 12, 2006, at 5:08 p.m. at the Carrefour store in Meylan, paid for with Susan Smith of Grenoble's bank card passed through the chip reader's field at Grand-Place today at 8:42 a.m., yesterday at 11:20 a.m., and last Monday at 9:05 a.m. It is joined by the book *30 Recipes for Family Weight-Loss*, borrowed from the city library by Gisèle Chabert," and so on.

The transponders have already entered the daily lives of many Parisians: the 'Navigo' passes that Autonomous Transit Authority of Paris (RATP) clients use to travel around allow the company to know exactly what route each passenger has followed. A transponder could also be associated with passports. George Monbiot envisions that authorities equipped with adequate material could verify the identity of each person in an entire crowd, during a demonstration, for example, with the country's new identity cards that include a transponder.

Even better, from the perspective of surveillance, the transponder could be carried in a person's body. Implantation has already replaced tattooing and is normal for pets. We're not quite there yet for humans, but that's coming: some faithful clients of the Baja Beach Club in Rotterdam have enthusiastically had transponders the size of a grain of rice implanted in their arms, which allows them to enter without being questioned by the bouncers and to not to have to pay their tabs—the chip reader debits their account automatically—as well as to spend time in the 'privileged persons' space. Other uses are appearing: two employees of the Citywatcher Company in Ohio were the first in the United States to have electronic microchips implanted as a means of identification to enter certain rooms in the company. In the United States, the director of Verychip, the company that manufactures the majority of implantable transponders, proposes they be implanted in legal immigrants so they can avoid any problems with the police.

Governments, moreover, are developing biometric identification, a process through which a person is recognized by digitally recording one of his physical characteristics on a card, such as his fingerprints or the form of his iris. Biometric recording on identity documents is becoming a common practice under the impetus of the United States. It could also be coupled with a transponder.

Thus, in its initial version the proposed INES identity card in France includes both a biometric element and a transponder.

An alternative to a microchip implant is the electronic bracelet linked to a global positioning system (GPS) locator. Some prisoners will soon be equipped with this bracelet. They could travel freely in areas determined in advance, with any transgression noted by the GPS and setting off an alarm in the control computer located with the supervisors.

But there's a much simpler solution, which is to use an infallible tracking device, with which the majority of citizens have equipped themselves with an enthusiasm that testifies to the vitality of the desire for imitation and emulation Veblen described: the cell phone. This device constitutes an excellent means for the authorities to track people: they can be located at any time by the relay antenna they are closest to. Consumers are getting so used to this permanent surveillance that they are being invited to indulge in it themselves: several companies offer parents the knowledge of where their children are at all times thanks to their cell phones, either through tracking by the relay antenna—with the telephone company passing on its information—or by a GPS tracking device built into the phone. One U.S. company, Verizon, even allows parents to programme the territories their little darlings are allowed to frequent. When the children leave the permitted area, their parents receive a warning message.

Betrayal by the Media

The media play an essential role in the dereliction of the democratic spirit. Either they relay the government's safety discourse, or distract public attention towards other matters, or they downplay the tendencies they observe by giving them scant visibility.

There are solid structural reasons, which we shall examine, for this media desertion. But it would be a mistake to neglect the imperceptible slide of the journalistic mind toward all-pervading conventional wisdom. One ends up finding all sorts of reasons to accept the established order. Indignation has become bad taste; divergent thinking is characterized as 'militancy'; criticism of the powerful is an antique trope of the journalistic art that one praises all the more fervently for indulging in it less.

The recent era has offered two episodes that constitute case studies for evaluating this development. Since September 11, 2001, the U.S. press has outdone itself by its lack of critical thinking with respect to the Bush administration. Swallowing the Patriot Act like mother's milk, it has sometimes outdone itself in the realm of the odious: was it not a so-called liberal weekly, *Newsweek*, that recommended the use of torture? But the press hit rock bottom when the Washington government spread reams of false intelligence during the 2002–03 winter to push for the invasion of Iraq, and the media never seriously questioned any of it. "I believe the press was muzzled and that it muzzled itself," declared Christiane Armanpour, CNN's 'star' reporter, in September 2003. "The entire political world, I mean the administration, the intelligence services, reporters, didn't ask enough questions."

Television stations and the majority of the print media ratified the official allegations that the Iraqi head of state supported the al-Qaeda network and was developing 'weapons of mass destruction'. The ornament and paragon of the print media, the *New York Times*, confirmed the presidential team's lies with all its weight. It twice, in September 2002 and April 2003, placed long 'investigative' stories on its front page that confirmed the official lies, in spite of the absence of solid evidence. It has since apologized, but the evil has been done.

If the supposedly best fell for it, how could the others have resisted the pull? A study of 1,600 television news broadcasts' coverage of the three-week war in April 2003 showed that, of all the points of view broadcast in interviews or commentaries, only 3 percent were in opposition to the war, which was a flagrant lack of balance, for polls indicated that 27 percent of people surveyed were opposed to the invasion of Iraq.

Let us not throw the first stone at our U.S. colleagues. The French press distinguished itself in the spring of 2005 in another kind of denial of the obvious and upholding of dominant thinking without any critical questioning. During the public debate that preceded the referendum on the proposed European Constitution, most of the media gave far more than the majority of their coverage to partisans for the yes vote, although it was obvious on the one hand that a large part of the population wanted to vote no, and on the other hand that the arguments of the opponents to the plan were based on well-substantiated reasoning. The most prestigious papers set the tone. Alas! These papers—or rather their management—did not see that this return of political debate was the sign of citizens' investment in the *res publica*, and that the media's role was to serve as the forum for that debate, to give an equal say to each side with enthusiasm and ardor, to illustrate in practice the virtues of democratic debate. But they, blind to the currents flowing in society, preferred to override the partisans of rejection—that is, the sovereign people, as the ballot results revealed on May 29, 2005—with insults (xenophobia, nationalism, dogmatism, and so on).

A strange thing resulted: many readers deemed it disagreeable to pay €1.30 every day (the cost of *Le Monde* or *Libération*) to be regarded as fascists. So they stopped doing it.

A major cause of the waning of the media's moral sense is that their directors and hierarchy most often echo the oligarchy's mode of thinking, since they feel themselves to be full members of it. High salaries seem normal to them, a chauffeured car the most natural thing in the world, and they passionately follow the customs of the ruling class. Here's what the high-society chronicler wrote about the sumptuous party the billionaire Pinault gave in Venice: "All the press barons, each with his spouse on his arm, as well as the owners of radio and television channels" were there.

The director names the editor-in-chief, who designates the different services' editors, who manage the reporters. Who chooses the director? The media owner. Although it does happen that he has a passion for the news and for freedom, the owner is more frequently guided by his own interests. In Hong Kong, for example, "out of the city's thirty daily papers, only the *Apple Daily* is independent and criticizes Beijing," says MP Martin Lee. "Why? Because its owner has no interests in China. All the others have invested in the mainland and don't want to lose money."

Capitalism No Longer Needs Democracy

How is the normalization of torture, multiplication of security laws, extensions of police powers, proliferation of surveillance instruments, and voluntary resignation of the press possible? How has such deterioration in the spirit of democracy come about? By virtue of the fact that, since the fall of the Soviet Union, the ruling class has become convinced that it no longer needs democracy. Before then, freedom was the best argument to counter the collectivist model. It was good for individuals and it promoted much greater economic success. But during the 1990s, the paradigm that linked freedom and capitalism dissolved. On the one hand, the extreme right, under the influence of 'neoconservatives', elaborated an ideology that made its priorities maintenance of the existing social order and of U.S. dominance. On the other hand, the impressive surge of the Chinese economy in a context of continual repression and one-party rule accustomed minds to a possible uncoupling of public freedoms and economic dynamism.

Thus democracy has become antithetical to the objectives the oligarchy seeks: democracy favours opposition to unwarranted privileges; it feeds doubts about illegitimate powers; it pushes for the rational examination of decisions. It is consequently more dangerous during a period when the harmful tendencies of capitalism are becoming more obvious.

On top of that, the maintenance of conspicuous waste involves a high level of oil and energy consumption. As the most important reserves are situated in the Middle East, a policy aimed at containing political subversion in that region must be conducted. That policy bears the name 'war against terror'. It presents the advantages of justifying restrictions on freedoms in the name of security, which allows repression of the social movements that are beginning to awaken.

The Desire for Catastrophe

Finally, I propose, as a subject for reflection, a provocative theory. We naïvely imagine that if they are aware of it at all, the rich dread the coming ecological catastrophe. They would feel powerless. But no. They desire it; they yearn for exacerbation, for disorder; they play at getting ever closer to the invisible edge of the volcano; they enjoy the excitement that obviously antisocial behaviour procures.

The manner in which President Bush's team launched the war in Iraq, the temptation—foiled up to now—to use nuclear mini-bombs in the framework of 'classic' warfare, and the upturn in U.S. military expenditures even though they already largely exceeded the sum total defence expenditures of the planet's most armed countries (Russia, China, France, Germany, Great Britain and India) can thus be read as the privileged class's drive toward a violent explosion. The temptation to catastrophe lurks in the minds of leaders. Thus we read in the *Wall Street Journal*, the United States' premier newspaper and the one most read by the oligarchy, these astonishing sentences from the pen of sociology professor Gunnar Heinsohn: "In some ways, the faster Europe collapses the better it will be for the U.S., whose chances of defeating global terrorism would improve by a panic-driven influx of the Old World's best, brightest and bravest ready to strengthen it economically and militarily."

One cannot exclude the possibility that some part of the oligarchy harbours an unconscious desire for catastrophe, pursues an apotheosis of consumption that would be the consumption of the planet Earth itself through exhaustion, through chaos, or through nuclear war. Violence is at the heart of the process on which a consumption society is based, Jean Baudrillard noted: "Using objects leads only to their slow loss. The value created by their violent loss is much more intense."

"The Era of Bitter Renunciations That Awaits Us"

However that may be, the coming crises, environmental and social, are going to subject our democratic system to severe tensions. To calm those tensions, we must meet the challenge posed by philosopher Hans Jonas in 1979: "It will be necessary to take measures that individual interests do not spontaneously impose and that may only with difficulty be the object of a democratic decision-making process." These measures amount to a policy easy to articulate but difficult to implement: reduce material consumption and agree to 'humanity's self-limitation' in the interest of all future generations.

But we cannot hope to reduce material consumption in a democratic society unless it is done equitably: pressure must first be brought to bear on the rich, which will cause it to be accepted—in negotiated forms—by the body of the people.

If the balance of power does not allow the imposition of this solution on the powerful, they will seek to maintain their excessive advantages by force, benefiting from the previous weakening of democracy and arguing that emergency measures are necessary. Governments have already tested this possibility with the state of emergency in France in the autumn of 2005, during the ghetto riots, and in the United States after Hurricane Katrina in September 2005, when the armed forces were sent—not to help the poor drowning people but to hunt down looters.

An irony of history could even be that an authoritarian government will trumpet the ecological necessity of restricting freedoms, without having to touch inequality. The management of epidemics, nuclear accidents, pollution peaks or the 'management' of climate-crisis emigrants are all motives that could facilitate the restriction of freedoms.

In the de Tocqueville text quoted from earlier, what makes the new despotism possible is individualism, self-absorption, and obliviousness to one's fellow citizens. That's precisely what capitalism promotes: its ideology exalts each person's pursuit of his own interests, claiming that the sum of individual behaviours leads by a sort of magic—'the invisible hand'—to an overall optimum.

To try to prevent these crises, we must, on the contrary, collectively decide on difficult choices; otherwise the disorders that will ensue will be met with a despotic response. We must urgently revitalize democracy, relegitimize concern for the common welfare, and reanimate the idea of collective destiny. Only in this way can we confront in freedom "the era of bitter requirements and renunciations that awaits us", to use Jonas's expression. Getting there includes anchoring social issues in ecology, articulating the imperative of solidarity in the reduction of consumption, and tenaciously reasserting that the only worthwhile existence—whatever the difficulties—is a free one.

6 | EMERGENCY AND OPTIMISM

There is an emergency. In less than a decade we will have to change course—assuming the collapse of the U.S. economy or the explosion of the Middle East does not impose a change through chaos.

To confront the emergency, we must understand the objective: to achieve a society that limits its material consumption; to plot the way there; to accomplish this transformation equitably, by first making those with the most carry the burden within and between societies; to take inspiration from collective values ascribed to here in France by amending our nation's motto to "Liberty, ecology, fraternity".

What are the main obstacles that block the way?

First of all, received wisdom—prejudices really—so loaded that they orient collective action without anyone really thinking about them.

The most powerful of these preconceived ideas is the belief in growth as the sole means of resolving social problems. That position is powerfully defended even as it is contradicted by the facts. And it is always defended by putting ecology aside because the zealots know that growth is incapable of responding to the environmental issue.

The second of these ideas, less cocky although very broadly disseminated, proclaims that technological progress will resolve environmental problems. This idea is propagated because it allows people to hope we will be able to avoid any serious changes in our collective behaviours thanks to technological progress. The development of technology, or rather of certain technical channels to the detriment of others, reinforces the system and fosters solid profits.

The third piece of received wisdom is the inevitability of unemployment. This idea is closely linked to the two previous ideas. Unemployment has become a given, largely manufactured by capitalism to assure the docility of the populace and especially of the lowest level of workers. From the opposite perspective, the transfer of the oligarchy's wealth for the purpose of public services, a system of taxation that weighed more heavily on pollution and on capital than on employment, sustainable agricultural policies in the countries of the South, and research into energy efficiency are all immense sources of employment.

A fourth idea commonly associates Europe and North America in a community of fortune. But their paths have diverged. Europe is still a standard-bearer for an ideal of universalism, the validity of which it demonstrates by its ability to unite—despite problems—very different states and cultures. Energy consumption, cultural values—for example, the critical significance of food—the rejection of the death penalty and torture, less pronounced inequality and the maintenance of an ideal of social justice, respect for international law, and support for the Kyoto Protocol on climate are some of the many traits that distinguish Europe from the United States. Europe must be separated from this overweening power and draw closer to the South, unless the United States shows it can really change.

The Oligarchy Could Be Divided

Then there are the forces at work.

The first, of course, is the power of the system itself. The failures that will occur will not in themselves be sufficient to undo the system, since, as we have seen, they could offer the pretext to promote an authoritarian system divested of any show of democracy. The social movement has woken up, however, and may continue to gain power. But it alone will not be able to carry the day in the face of the rise of repression: it will be necessary for the middle classes and part of the oligarchy—which is not monolithic—to clearly take sides for public freedoms and the common good.

The mass media constitute a central challenge. Today they support capitalism because of their own economic situation. They depend, for the most part, on advertising. That makes it difficult for them to plead for a reduction in consumption. On top of that, the development of free papers that depend solely on advertising further increases the pressure on widely distributed paid newspapers, many of which have entered the stables of big industrial groups. It's not certain that the information possibilities generated by the Internet, although immense—and for as long as these remain open—will be adequate to counterbalance the weight of the mass media should it wholly become the voice of the oligarchy. Nevertheless, not all journalists are totally subservient yet, and they could be galvanized around the ideal of freedom.

The third, wobbly force is the left. Since its social-democratic component became its centre of gravity, it has abandoned any ambition of transforming the world. The compromise with free-market liberalism has led the left to so totally adopt the values of free-market liberalism that it no longer dares—except in the most cautious terms—to deplore social inequality. On top of that, the left displays an almost cartoonish refusal to truly engross itself in environmental issues. The left remains pickled in the idea of progress as it was conceived in the nineteenth century, still believes that science is produced the same way it was in the time of Albert Einstein, and intones the chant of economic growth without the slightest trace of critical thinking. Moreover, 'social capitalism' rather than 'social democracy' is undoubtedly the more apposite term. But can the challenges of the twenty-first century be addressed by the currents of a movement other than the one that identified inequality as its primary motive for revolt? This hiatus is at the heart of political life. The left will be reborn by uniting the causes of inequality and the environment—or, unfit, it will disappear in the general disorder that will sweep it and everything else away.

And yet, let us be optimistic. Optimistic, because there are ever more of us who understand—unlike all the conservatives—the historical novelty of the situation: we are living out a new, never-seen-before phase of the human species' history, the moment when, having conquered the Earth and reached its limits, humanity must rethink its relationship to nature, to space, to its destiny.

We are optimistic to the extent that awareness of the importance of the current stakes becomes ever more pervasive, to the extent that the spirit of freedom and of solidarity is aroused. Since Seattle and the protests against the World Trade Organization in 1999, the pendulum has begun to swing in the other direction, towards a collective concern about the choices for the future, seeking cooperation rather than competition. The somewhat successful—although still incomplete—battle in Europe against GMOs, the international community's continuance of the Kyoto Protocol in 2001 despite the United States' withdrawal, the refusal by the peoples of Europe to participate in the invasion of Iraq in 2003, and the general recognition of the urgency of climate-change challenge are signs that the wind of the future has begun to blow. Despite the scale of the challenges that await us, solutions are emerging and—faced with the sinister prospects that the oligarchs promote—the desire to remake the world is being reborn.

EPILOGUE | AT THE PLANET CAFÉ

It would be bad to end on too sombre a note. For after all, we are joyful, like our friend Lovelock, and believe that a certain lightness of spirit will help dissolve the disastrous scenarios the leaden-soled oligarchs have written.

A few decades ago, the first billionaire in France, Marcel Dassault, regularly delivered a 'business café' in his weekly magazine, in which he staged a conversation between good people who expressed the concerns of the moment, as Dassault understood them. I no longer remember what he said there very well, but the form was original. In tribute to Uncle Marcel—you see that I mean no harm to billionaires; we must just divide their fortunes by a hundred or a thousand and establish an indispensable maximum allowable income (MAI)—here's a new 'Planet Café'. I asked various comrades met by chance in my reading for help:

FÉLIX GUATTARI, psychiatrist: Without humanity radically taking itself in hand, we risk there being no further human history.

• *You're certainly not afraid of big statements. There's no catastrophe yet, all the same!*

JEAN-PIERRE DUPUY, philosopher: If we are to prevent the catastrophe, we need to believe in the possibility of it happening before it does.

• *And what, for example, could happen if we don't?*

ROBERT BARBAULT, ecologist: If humanity does not plot out radically new ways to conduct its affairs between now and

2050, then the outlook is grim and the sixth-extinction crisis a certain prospect.

• *So, no more frogs. That's it?*

KOFI ANNAN, former United Nations secretary-general: In Africa over the course of the next twenty years, some 60 million people will leave the Sahel region for less hostile places if the desertification of their lands is not arrested.

• *Ah, now I get it. . . . They'll come here, is that it? I don't like that so much. We'll close the borders; we'll protect ourselves!*

HAMA AMADOU, prime minister of Niger: No measure, no army of police and troops, will be able to prevent our citizens who are prey to poverty and hunger from invading the lands of abundance.

• *Now that's getting hot. We're not going to imprison the whole world, all the same. These countries must develop; there has to be economic growth; that's the only solution. If they've got grub at home, they won't come for ours.*

LESTER BROWN, agronomist: If China reaches the level of three cars for four people, as in the United States, it will count 1.1 billion cars. Today, there are only 800 million cars in the whole world. That would require 99 million barrels of oil a day. Today, the world produces 82 million barrels a day.

• *You're telling me there won't be enough oil, OK. Yeah, it's already enough to make you crazy at the pump. But you see, it's China and India that aggravate the problem. They're already producing a ton of your greenhouse gases. Let them do something about it, after all!*

LAURENCE TUBIANA, director of the International Institute for Sustainable Development: First World countries must allow emerging countries access to resources: far from competing for that access, they must strongly restrain their own consumption of natural resources. That's the only responsible attitude that will allow emerging countries to rethink the growth model they are going to borrow as legitimate and equitable.

• *"Restrain our consumption", as though you think it's easy. We have poor people too.*

MARTIN HIRSCH, president of Emmaus, France: It's illusory to hope to conquer poverty in rich countries without dealing with poor countries' poverty.

• *Oh well, you all agree; it's not possible to have a discussion! OK, well, me too, I'm going to repeat myself: growth in poor countries is necessary!*

JUAN SOMAVIA, director general of the International Labour Organization: At the global level, unemployment has increased 21.9 percent in ten years, affecting 191.8 million people in 2005, a historic record. China, which enjoys an annual growth rate of between 9 and 10 percent, creates about 10 million new jobs each year, two times less than the number of people who enter the country's workforce.

• *Oh, that's enough! It's fine to criticize growth, but do you have another solution?*

DAMIEN MILLET, from the Committee for the Abolition of Third World Debt: The absolute priority must be the universal satisfaction of the most fundamental human needs.

• *That's not a solution!*

AN FAO AGRONOMIST: Judicious agricultural policies combined with a good level of investment could help reduce the pressure from illegal immigration that is forcing open the doors to Europe and North America.

• *A good level of investment? You're talking about real money there. And where are you going to find it?*

A UNDP EXPERT: The sum necessary to bring a billion people across the poverty threshold of $1 a day is $300 billion. As an absolute amount, this number appears exorbitant.

Nonetheless, it equals less than 2 percent of the income of the richest 10 percent of the global population.

• *And you think they're going to let go of their 2 percent just like that? Aren't you a little naïve?*

ROBERT NEWMAN, author of *History of Oil*: Corporations will prevent any law or regulation that seeks to constrain their profitability. It's only by breaking the power of the big firms and by subjecting them to social control that we will be able to surmount the environmental crisis.

• *Well, I wish you joy. The Englishman is right; the bosses at Coca-Cola and company are not going to let somebody swipe their sirloin to win the good graces of the starving masses.*

MICHAEL MOORE, filmmaker: The only true value your life has to the wealthy is that they need your vote every election day in order to get the politicians they've funded into office. They can't do that by themselves. This damnable system of ours that allows for the country to be run by the will of the people is a rotten deal for them as they represent only 1 percent of 'the people'.

• *Moore's the fat anti-Bush guy, right? Yeah, he was at the Cannes festival and I saw him on TV. He's a riot. Except, I don't know whether you've ever noticed it, but we don't actually all vote the same way. And then the left, which is sort of against the rich, well it's finally also for growth. And wham!*

GENEVIÈVE AZAM, economist: Asserting a political ecology is the necessary condition for the social and the environmental questions to be posed at the same time. The choices and the modalities of wealth production and distribution cannot be considered separately.

• *Hoo ha! An intellectual, that one! "Cannot be considered separately." Me, I want something concrete!*

JEAN MATOUK, economist: In a big company where the

salaries of the twenty most senior executives total $12 million, a 20 percent reduction of those salaries allows the creation, within the company itself or a subsidiary, of fifty new jobs at a monthly salary of $2,200. The number of jobs created this way is small, but it increases very rapidly if the reduction in salaries is extended down through all the strata to the level just above that one, even at a lower rate.

• *Oh, now that's a hoot; I like that. But all the same, if we reduce rich people's salaries, we'll have less stuff.*

HENRY MILLER, author: What we dread most, in facing the impending débâcle, is that we shall be obliged to give up our gew-gaws, our gadgets, all the little comforts which have made us so uncomfortable.

• *Baubles . . . we're back to Africa. I'm not sure you're right about everything, but you're a good guy. Come on, let's drink another glass; this round's on me! To the health of the planet!*

NOTES

PREFACE

xv A version of this preface originally appeared on Truthout.org on 15 March 2007.

CHAPTER 1

2 *we deem that the rate of extinction*   Michel Loreau's statements quoted in Hervé Kempf, "A Mass Species Extinction Is Foreseen for the XXIst Century," *Le Monde,* 9 January 2006.

3 *With global warming*   Hervé Kempf, "James Lovelock, docteur catastrophe," *Le Monde,* 11 February 2006. See also Lovelock's *The Revenge of Gaia* (London: Allen Lane, 2006).

4 *An intense discussion among scientists followed*   Alfred Sauvy discusses it in *Croissance zéro?* (Paris: Calmann-Lévy, 1973), 197.

4 *increase in average temperature*   Intergovernmental Panel on Climate Change (IPCC), *Climate Change 2001: Synthesis Report for Decision-Makers*, 9.

6 *which climatologists place at around 2 degrees*   *Report of the Steering Committee*, International Symposium on the Stabilization of Greenhouse Gases, Hadley Centre, Met Office, Exeter, England, 1–3 February 2005.

6 *this restorative process could no longer take place*   See "La menace de l'emballement," *Science et Vie*, no. 1061 (February 2006).

6 *a half metre of rise*   Richard Kerr, "A Worrying Trend of Less Ice, Higher Seas," *Science* 311 (24 March 2006): 1698.

7 *Europe's vegetation*   Philippe Ciais et al., "Europe-wide Reduction in Primary Productivity Caused by the Heat and Drought in 2003," *Nature*, 22 September 2005.

7 *All the carbon recently stored*   Sergey Zimov et al., "Permafrost and the Global Carbon Budget," *Science* 312 (16 June 2006): 1612–1613.

7 *climate models have underestimated the interactions*   Marten Scheffer et al., "Positive Feedback between Global Warming and Atmospheric CO_2 Concentration Inferred from Past Climate Change," *Geophysical Letters* 33 (2006).

7 *Eight degrees of warming*   Stephen Schneider, e-mail message to author, 24 March 2006. See also Stephen Schneider and Michael Mastrandea,

"Probabilistic Assessment of 'Dangerous' Climate Change and Emissions Pathways," *PNAS*, 1 November 2005.

8 *since the dinosaurs disappeared 65 million years ago*   "Humans Spur Worst Extinctions Since Dinosaurs," Reuters, 21 March 2006.

8 *threatened species 'red list'*   Hervé Morin, "L'érosion de la diversité biologique de la planète se poursuit," *Le Monde*, 23 May 2005.

8 *substantial decline in the abundance*   "Mapping Human Impacts on the Biosphere," www.globio.info, consulted March 2006.

9 *more land has been converted to agriculture since 1950*   Millenium Ecosystem Assessment, *Living beyond Our Means: Statement from the Board*, March 2005.

9 *We have experienced more rapid change in the last thirty years*   Neville Ash (World Conservation Centre, Cambridge, England), personal communication, June 2005. See also UNEP, *One Planet, Many People: Atlas of Our Changing Environment* (Nairobi, 2005).

9 *the group Demonstrate for Landscapes*   www.manifestepourlespaysages.org

10 *Jacques Weber*   Cited by Philippe Testard-Vaillant, "Biodiversité. Les cinq défis du CNRS," *Le Figaro*, 28 April 2006.

10 *Jean-Pierre Féral*   Ibid.

11 *reduction in fishing catches*   FAO, *State of World Fisheries and Aquaculture*, 2005.

11 *three kilograms of garbage for every half kilogram of plankton*   Kristina Gjerde, *Ecosystems and Biodiversity in Deep Waters and High Seas*, UNEP-UICN, 2006.

11 *wild salmon pollute the immaculate lakes*   E. M. Krümmel et al., "Delivery of Pollutants by Spawning Salmon," *Nature*, 18 September 2003.

12 *In Germany*   BUND and Friends of the Earth, Europe, *Toxic Inheritance* (www.foeeurope.org/publications/2006/toxic_inheritance.pdf, 2006).

12 *link between exposure to low doses of insecticide*   John Meeker et al., "Exposure to Nonpersistent Insecticides and Male Reproductive Hormones," *Epidemiology*, January 2006.

12 *atmospheric pollution . . . affects human reproduction*   Rémy Slama, "Les polluants de l'air influencent-ils la reproduction humaine?" *Extrapol*, no. 28 (June 2006).

13 *the lengthening of life expectancy*   Claude Aubert, *Espérance de vie, la fin des illusions* (Mens, France: Terre vivante, 2006).

13 *women's life expectancy has moved towards a plateau*   Jean-Claude Chesnais (INED), personal communication, June 2006.

13 *Jay Olshansky*   Jay Olshansky, "A Potential Decline in Life Expectancy in the United States in the 21st century," *The New England Journal of Medicine* 352, no. 11 (2005): 1138.

14 *in 2004, China emitted*   Energy Information Administration, *International Energy Annual 2004*; European Environment Agency, *Annual European Community Greenhouse Gas Inventory 1990–2004 and Inventory Report 2006.*

14 *in 2003, it used 1.2 times that capacity*   World Wildlife Fund, *Living Planet Report 2006.*

15 *In China, the loss of arable land*   Worldwatch Institute, *State of the World 2006* (Geneva: Association L'état de la planète publications, 2006), 17.

15 *The desert advances*   "China Promises to Push Back Spreading Deserts," Reuters, 1 March 2006.

15 *Every spring, the Yellow River*   Frédéric Koller, "Chine: le mal paysan," *Alternatives économiques*, February 2006.

15 *Three hundred million Chinese . . . drink polluted water*   Richard McGregor, "The Polluter Pays: How Environmental Disaster Is Straining China's Social Fabric," *Financial Times*, 27 January 2006.

15 *pollution in the Yangtze*   "Cri d'alarme des experts face à la pollution du Yangtse," Agence France Presse, 30 May 2006.

15 *Twenty of the thirty cities*   Lindsay Beck, "China Warns of Disaster If Pollution Not Curbed," Reuters, 13 March 2006.

15 *Chinese air is so saturated*   Worldwatch Institute, *The State of the World 2006*, 8.

16 *weakening the ability of coral and plankton*   Peter Haugan et al., *Effects on the Marine Environment of Ocean Acidification Resulting from Elevated Levels of CO_2 in the Atmosphere* (Oslo: Directorate for Nature Management, 2006).

16 *organisms that have a shell*   Stéphane Foucart, "L'océan de plus en plus acide," *Le Monde,* 18 and 19 June 2006. See also EUR-Océans, "L'acidification des océans: un nouvel enjeu pour la recherche et le réseau d'excellence Eur-Océans," 1 June 2006.

16 *a scientific study published in 2004* Chris Thomas et al., "Extinction Risk from Climate Change," *Nature* 427 (2004): 145.

17 *the nuclear-power lobby* This was signaled as early as 1989 in "Effet de serre: l'alibi nucléaire," *Reporterre*, September 1989.

17 *Hubbert's Peak* Jean-Luc Wingert, *La Vie après le pétrole* (Paris: Autrement, 2005).

18 *China today consumes one-thirteenth* Adapted from Worldwatch Institute, *State of the World 2006*, 11, corrected by the author with statistics from *BP Statistical Review of World Energy*, June 2006.

18 *in 2007 for the most pessimistic* Wingert, *La Vie après le pétrole*, 90.

18 *around 2040 or 2050* Ibid., 98.

18 *The Total Oil Company* Hervé Kempf, "Selon Total, la production de pétrole culminera vers 2025," *Le Monde*, 19 June 2004.

19 *According to Michel Loreau* Michel Loreau, "Une extinction massive des espèces est annoncée pour le XXIe siècle," *Le Monde*, 9 January 2006.

19 *Martin McKee* Martin McKee, "Prévenir et combattre l'éternel retour des épidémies," statements gathered by Laure Belot and Paul Benkimoun, *Le Monde*, 2 and 3 April 2006.

20 *Yves Cochet* Cited by Hervé Kempf, "Écologisme radical et décroissance," *Le Monde,* 4 March 2005. See also Yves Cochet, *Pétrole Apocalypse* (Paris: Fayard, 2005).

20 *Two engineers, Jean-Marc Jancovici* Jean-Marc Jancovici and Alain Grandjean, *Le plein s'il vous plaît!* (Paris: Éditions du Seuil, 2005), 124.

24 *it has been has been incapable of integrating* See Jean-Paul Besset, *Comment ne plus être progressiste . . . sans devenir réactionnaire* (Paris: Fayard, 2005).

CHAPTER 2

30 *In the the course of the winter of 2005–06* Bertrand Bissuel, "La fréquentation des centres pour sans-abri a augmenté significativement," *Le Monde*, 22 April 2006.

30 *More and more people in France live in trailers* According to Claire Cossée, of the CNRS, cited by Christelle Chabaud, "Caravanes de la précarité," *L'Humanité Hebdo*, 14 and 15 January 2006.

30 *more than 120 million children* Hubert Prolongeau, "Des enfants dans la rue," www.lattention.com, consulted in April 2006.

30   *In 2004 in France, close to 3.5 million people*   Cyril Hofstein, "Ces hommes et ces femmes à la dérive," *Le Figaro*, 28 April 2006.

31   *According to the National Observatory*   Cyrille Poy, "Un bilan très alarmant," *L'Humanité Hebdo*, 25 and 26 February 2006.

31   *At the beginning of 2006*   Ibid.

31   *In Switzerland, the Caritas association*   Damien Roustel, "La pauvreté gagne du terrain en Suisse," *L'Humanité*, 12 January 2006.

31   *In Germany, the proportion of people*   Odile Benyahia- Kouider, "Aveu de pauvreté," *Libération*, 16 September 2005.

31   *In Great Britain, it reached 22 percent*   Eldin Fahmy and David Gordon, "La pauvreté et l'exclusion sociale en Grande-Bretagne," *Économie et Statistique*, nos. 383–85 (2005): 110.

31   *In the United States, 23 percent*   Jacques Mistral, "Aux États-Unis, il n'y a pas d'exclus, il y a des pauvres," *Alternatives économiques*, May 2006.

32   *In Japan, "the number of households*   Philippe Pons, "La hausse des inégalités crée un Japon à deux vitesses," *Le Monde*, 3 May 2006.

32   *while several dozen employees*   Christine Garin, "Des agents de la Ville de Paris se retrouvent sans domicile fixe," *Le Monde*, 19 September 2005.

32   *As economist Jacques Rigaudiat explains*   Jacques Rigaudiat, "20 millions de précaires en France," statement cited by Cyrille Poy, *L'Humanité*, 3 March 2006.

32   *The ONPES confirms*   Poy, "Un bilan très alarmant."

32   *Pierre Concialdi*   Pierre Concialdi, "Between 1.3 and 3.6 million poor workers," statements reported by Christelle Chabaud, *L'Humanité Hebdo*, 14 and 15 January 2006.

32   *According to Labor Minister Franz Müntefering*   Franz Müntefering, interview in the *Financial Times Deutschland*, 3 April 2005.

32   *According to the Alarm Network on Inequalities*   Réseau d'alerte sur les inégalités, "Baromètre des inégalités et de la pauvreté, édition 2006: Bip40 poursuit sa hausse," 2006, www.bip40.org.

32   *French Institute for Economic Statistics*   Michel Delberghe, "Selon l'INSEE, le pouvoir d'achat des ménages a augmenté de 1,4 percent en 2004," *Le Monde*, 11 November 2005, citing INSEE, *France, Portrait social 2005–2006*, November 2005.

33   *There's been a switch in the trend*   Louis Maurin, personal communication, June 2006.

33 *The borders of poverty are becoming blurred*   Martin Hirsch, "Les formes modernes de la pauvreté," in *La Nouvelle Critique sociale* (Paris: Éditions du Seuil, 2006), 78.

33 *For Jacques Rigaudiat*   Rigaudiat, "20 millions de précaires en France."

33 *notes the United Nations Development Program*   UNDP, *Human Development Report 2005* (Economica, 2005), 3, 4.

33 *2.4 billion don't have proper sanitation*   UNDP, *L'Avenir de l'environnement mondial 3 (GEO 3)* (De Boeck Université, 2002), 152.

34 *Life expectancy is increasing*   Ibid., 33, 21.

34 *extreme poverty has receded*   Ibid., 22.

34 *The share of the population*   Worldwatch Institute, *L'État 2006 de la planète*, 6.

34 *Similarly, China has reduced*   FAO, *State of the World Food Security*, 2003.

34 *Since the mid-1990s*   UNDP, *Human Development Report 2005*, 37.

34 *was estimated at 800 million*   FAO, *L'État de l'insécurité alimentaire dans le monde 2003* (2003).

34 *while 2 billion human beings*   Marcel Mazoyer, quoted by Hervé Kempf, "Alerte pour 800 millions d'hommes sous-alimentés," *Le Monde*, 10 June 2002.

34 *Even India is seeing the number*   FAO, *L'État de l'insécurité alimentaire dans le monde 2005* (2005), 30.

34 *"This development,"*   Quoted by Hervé Kempf, "La faim dans le monde augmente à nouveau," *Le Monde*, 27 November 2003.

34 *More recent statistics confirm*   AFP, "Chances of halving world hunger by 2015 remote", September 18, 2008.

35 *a billion of the world's city dwellers*   UN-Habitat, *State of the World's Cities 2006/7* (Earthscan, 2006), ix.

35 *In France, according to INSEE*   Delberghe, "Selon l'INSEE, le pouvoir d'achat."

35 *for the last twenty years, average wage conditions*   Pierre Concialdi, "Entre 1,3 et 3,6 millions de travailleurs pauvres," statements quoted by Christelle Chabaud, *L'Humanité Hebdo*, 14 and 15 January 2006.

36 *For economist Thomas Piketty*   Thomas Piketty, *L'Économie des inégalités* (Paris: Editions La Découverte, 2004), 19.

36 *In fact, a study conducted by Piketty* Thomas Piketty and Emmanuel Saez, "The Evolution of Top Incomes: A Historical and International Perspective," NBER Working Papers, no. W11955 (January 2006).

36 *in the United States* "Even Higher Society, Ever Harder to Ascend," *Economist*, 29 December 2004.

36 *Inequality has grown regularly* Dan Seligman, "The Inequality Imperative," *Forbes*, 10 October 2005, 64.

36 *In Japan up until the beginning of the 1990s* Philippe Pons, "Adachi: un cas de paupérisation silencieuse," *Le Monde*, 3 May 2006.

36 *At this time, "inequalities have begun to widen* Pons, "La hausse des inégalités."

37 *In the middle of the 1950s* Louis Maurin, "La société de l'inégalité des chances," *Alternatives économiques*, February 2006.

37 *notes sociologist Louis Chauvel* Louis Chauvel, "Déclassement: les jeunes en première ligne," *Alternatives économiques*, special issue, no. 69 (3rd trimester, 2006): 50.

37 *The disparities in capital are far greater* Piketty, *L'Économie des inégalités*, 14.

37 *If, with respect to purchasing power* Hervé Nathan et al., "Ceux qui possèdent la France," *Marianne*, 26 August 2006.

38 *In Guatemala in 1997* Henriette Geiger (European Union representative in Guatemala), personal communication, October 2001.

38 *Generally, Latin America and Africa* UNDP, *Human Development Report 2005*, 38, 53.

38 *In India* Ibid., 32.

38 *In China* François Lantz, "Chine: les faiblesses d'une puissance," *Alternatives économiques*, March 2006.

38 *A Chinese boss, Zhang Xin* Quoted by Maria Bartiromo, "What They Said at Davos," *Business Week*, 6 February 2006.

39 *According to the UNDP* UNDP, *Human Development Report 2005*, 27.

39 *Not only have the poorest countries "not been able* Ibid., 39.

39 *The South "cannot dampen the negative effects* Sunita Narain, preface to *L'État 2006 de la planète,* Worldwatch Institute.

40 *notes André Cicolella* André Cicolella, "Santé sacrifiée," *Politis*, 13 April 2006.

41 *in China, warns Environment Minister Zhou Shenxian* "Pollution Fueling Social Unrest—Chinese Official," Reuters, 21 April 2006.

41 *dozens of 'cancer villages'* Philippe Grangereau, "Xiditou, 'village du cancer' sacrifié à la croissance chinoise," *Libération*, 11 April 2006.

41 *74,000 in 2004* Frédéric Koller, "Chine: le mal paysan," *Alternatives économiques*, February 2006.

41 *6 peasants killed by the police* "Fat of the Land," *Economist*, 25 March 2006.

41 *in Brazil (39 murders in 2004)* According to the Pastoral Commission for the Land, cited by Reuters, "Brazil Land Conflicts Worst in Decades—Report," 20 April 2005.

42 *"In numerous cases," the experts of Millennium* Millennium Ecosystem Assessment, *Living beyond Our Means: Statement from the Board*, March 2005, 19–20.

42 *two-thirds of those who subsist* UNDP, *Report on Human Development 2005*, 10.

43 *as agronomist Marc Dufumier notes* Marc Dufumier, "Pour une émigration choisie: le commerce équitable," unpublished, May 2006. See Marc Dufumier, *Agriculture et Paysanneries des Tiers mondes* (Paris: Karthala, 2004).

CHAPTER 3

44 *oligarchy* *Webster's Tenth New Collegiate Dictionary*.

44 *the U.S. 'robber barons'* Marianne Debouzy, *Le Capitalisme "sauvage" aux États-Unis, 1860–1900* (Paris: Éditions du Seuil, 1972).

44 *Between 2000 and 2004, the remuneration* Jean-Claude Jaillette et al., "Revenus 1995–2005. Les gagnants et les perdants," *Marianne*, 4 March 2006.

44 *according to the consulting firm Proxinvest* Proxinvest, press release, "Rapport 2005 sur la rémunération des dirigeants des sociétés cotées," 22 November 2005.

44 *the best-paid bosses in France* Bruno Declairieux, "Salaires des patrons: encore une année faste!" *Capital*, December 2005.

44 *Since 1998, the remuneration* Thierry Philippon, "Monsieur 250 millions d'euros," *Le Nouvel Observateur*, 8 June 2006.

45 *on other companies' boards of directors, and so on* Ibid.

45 *according to a Standard and Poor's study* Adam Geller, "Rise in Pay for CEOs Slows but Doesn't Stop," *International Herald Tribune*, 20 April 2006.

45 *the Sunoco boss*   Ibid.; Alex Tarquinio, "Oil Prices Push Upward, and Bosses' Pay Follows," *New York Times*, covered by *Le Monde*, 22 April 2006.

46 *In 1989, Peugeot CEO*   Jean-Luc Porquet, *Que les gros salaires baissent la tête!* (Paris: Editions Michalon, 2005), 16.

46 *management guru Peter Drucker*   Quoted by Laure Belot and Martine Orange, "Les avis de Peter Drucker et Warren Buffet," *Le Monde*, 23 May 2003.

46 *Between 1995 andw 2005, income*   Jean-Claude Jaillette et al., "Revenus 1995–2005: Les gagnants et les perdants," *Marianne*, 4 March 2006.

47 *This profit is not the result*   Robert Rochefort, "La France, un pays riche!," *La Croix*, 16 January 2006.

47 *3,000 of the city's bankers*   Marc Roche, "3000 banquiers de la City auront un bonus de plus de 1 million de livres," *Le Monde*, 31 December 2005.

47 *The investment banking firm Goldman Sachs*   Ibid.

47 *Greenwich, Connecticut, near New York*   Stephen Schurr, "A Day in the Life of America's Financial Frontier Boom Town," Financial Times, 13 March 2006.

47 *says Philip Beresford*   Quoted by Agnès Catherine Poirier, "Par ici la money," *Télérama*, 3 May 2006.

47 *The increasing number of billionaires*   Luisa Kroll and Allison Fass, "Billionaire Bacchanalia," *Forbes*, 27 March 2006.

47 *a sum equal to*   CADTM, press release, "Le CADTM demande un impôt exceptionnel sur la fortune cumulée des 793 milliardaires distingués par *Forbes*," 10 March 2006.

47 *Another way of looking at it*   UNDP, *Human Development Report 2005*, 40.

48 *James Simons of Renaissance*   Stephen Taub, "Really Big Bucks," *Institutional Investor's Alpha*, May 2006, and Cécile Prudhomme, "Les 'hedge funds' enrichissent les 'papys' de la finance," *Le Monde*, 4 and 5 June 2006.

48 *Forbes counts 33 billionaires*   Kroll and Fass, "Billionaire Bacchanalia."

48 *And of the 8.7 million millionaires*   Hervé Rousseau, "Les riches, toujours plus riches et plus nombreux," *Le Figaro*, 21 June 2006; Maguy Day, "Le nombre des très riches a crû de 500 000 dans le monde en 2005," *Le Monde,* 23 June 2006.

48 *In the countries of the former Soviet Union* Jacques Amalric, "La Russie, propriété de Poutine," *Alternatives internationales*, June 2006; Eric Chol, "Les oligarques débarquent," *L'Express*, 15 June 2006.

48 *As one Russian commentator observed* Vladimir Volkov, "*Forbes*'s Billionaires List and the Growth of Inequality in Russia," www.wsws .org, 3 April 2006.

49 *Lakshmi Mittal* François Labrouillère, "Le Meccano du roi de l'acier Mittal," *Paris-Match*, 4 May 2006.

49 *In Germany, employers convinced* Odile Benyahia-Kouider, "Aveu de pauvreté," *Libération*, 16 September 2005.

49 *Prime Minister Junichiro Koizumi* Pons, "La hausse des inégalités."

49 *According to the French Observatory of Economic Cycles* Cited by Maurin, "La société de l'inégalité des chances,"

50 *According to a study by the Urban Institute* Cited by Éric Leser, "Le Congrès prolonge les baisses d'impôts sur les dividendes," *Le Monde*, 13 May 2005.

50 *If there is no justice* Augustine, *The City of God*, 4.4.

51 *George Bush is the son* "Even Higher Society, Ever Harder to Ascend," *Economist*, 29 December 2004.

51 *when, for example, Mr. Pinault* Henri-Jean Servat, "François Pinault, L'invitation au palais," *Paris-Match*, 4 May 2006.

52 *At Harvard University* "Even Higher Society, Ever Harder to Ascend."

52 *In Japan, people deplore* Pons, "Adachi: un cas de paupérisation silencieuse."

52 *This story recounted in* Forbes Kiri Blakeley, "Bigger Than Yours," *Forbes*, 27 March 2006.

52 *The* Octopus *in question* Nathalie Funès and Corinne Tissier, "Leur incroyable mode de vie," *Le Nouvel Observateur*, 24 November 2005.

52 *The French hyper-rich* Ibid.

53 *Here are a few things* Forbes "The Price of Living Well," *Forbes*, 10 October 2005.

53 *that one may squander $241,000 in a night* Eugenia Levenson, "The Weirdiest CEO Moments of 2005," *Fortune*, 12 December 2005.

53 *install air-conditioning* Nathalie Brafman and Pierre-Antoine Delhommais, "Le club des très riches se mondialise," *Le Monde*, 15 December 2005.

53 *the Bentley 728* Dexter Roberts and Frederik Balfour, "To Get Rich Is Glorious," *Business Week*, 6 February 2006.

53 *the Koenigsegg CCR* "Inproducts," *Business Week*, 19 June 2006.

53 *the Chang An Club* Roberts and Balfour, "To Get Rich Is Glorious."

53 *a serious gym* Susan Yara, "Super Gyms for the Super Rich," *Forbes*, 27 April 2006.

53 *A well-off fellow like Joseph Jacobs* Schurr, "A Day in the Life."

53 *In Paris, Bernard Arnault* Yves Le Grix, "Dans les belles demeures, il n'y a pas de plafond," *Challenges*, 13 July 2006.

53 *David de Rothschild lives* Funès and Tissier, "Leur incroyable mode de vie."

53 *Silvio Berlusconi's property* "La Sardaigne taxe les riches," *Le Nouvel Observateur*, 11 May 2006.

53 *or Jean-Marie Fourtou's place* Jean-Pierre Tuquoi, *Majesté, je dois beaucoup à votre père* . . . (Paris: Albin Michel, 2006), 53, 136.

53 *The art collection* Funès and Tissier, "Leur incroyable mode de vie."

54 *a London banker describes* Roche, "3,000 banquiers de la City."

54 *Jacques Chirac at the Royal Palm* *Paris-Match*, 4 August 2000, quoted by Pascale Robert-Diard and Nicole Vulser, "*Paris-Match* présente ses excuses à M. Chirac," *Le Monde*, 5 August 2000.

54 *Closer to the people are* Vincent Giret and Véronique Le Billon, *Les Vies cachées de DSK* (Paris: Éditions du Seuil, 2000), 120.

55 *such as Thierry Breton* Funès and Tissier, "Leur incroyable mode de vie."

55 *It would be very important to fit out* "Les ailes coupées de la Sogerma," *L'Humanité*, 6 April 2006.

55 *the Falcon 900EX* Advertisement for Dassault-Falcon, "Leave Your Competition at the Fuel Truck," *Forbes*, 10 October 2005.

55 *It costs $20 million* Éric Leser, "Bientôt en librairie, le 'guide du touriste de l'espace,'" *Le Monde*, 2 November 2005.

55 *Virgin Galactic* Christine Ducros, "Décollage imminent pour le tourisme spatial," *Le Figaro*, 18 April 2006.

55 *the Phoenix that U.S. Subs offers* "US Submarines," in "How to Spend It," *Financial Times* supplement, June 2006.

55 *François Pinault invited*　　Servat, "François Pinault, L'invitation au palais."

56 *at his daughter Delphine's wedding*　　*Paris-Match*, 22 September 2005.

56 *the girls are named Chloé*　　Isabelle Cottenceau, "Jeunes, riches, un enfer!" *Paris-Match*, 4 May 2006.

56 *Paris Hilton*　　Laurence Caracalla, "Paris Hilton," *Le Figaro*, 28 April 2006; "C'est fini entre Paris Hilton et Stavros Niarchos," Associated Press, 3 May 2006.

57 *In the United States, they increasingly live*　　Corine Lesnes, "Dans les cités idéales de l'american way of life," *Le Monde 2*, 15 January 2005; Pascale Kremer, "À l'abri derrière les grilles," *Le Monde 2*, 26 November 2005.

57 *according to the National Association of Homebuilders*　　David Kocieniewski, "After an $8,000 Garage Makeover, There's Even Room for the Car," *New York Times*, reprinted in *Le Monde*, 18 March 2006.

57 *The phenomenon is being duplicated*　　Luis Felipe Cabrales Barajas, "Gated Communities Are Not the Solution to Urban Insecurity," in UN-Habitat, *State of the World's Cities 2006/7* (Earthscan, 2006), 146.

57 *Today, my fear is that security*　　Quoted by Kremer, "À l'abri derrière les grilles."

CHAPTER 4

60 *Raymond Aron, who was*　　Raymond Aron, "Avez-vous lu Veblen?" in Thorstein Veblen, *Théorie de la classe de loisir* (Paris: Gallimard, 1970), viii.

60 *He lived a retired, if rather eccentric, existence*　　Robert Heilbroner, *The Worldly Philosophers* (New York: Simon & Schuster, 1953).

60 *what historians called "untamed capitalism"*　　Marianne Debouzy, *Le Capitalisme "sauvage" aux États-Unis, 1860–1900* (Paris: Éditions du Seuil), 1972.

61 *"the propensity for emulation—for invidious comparison*　　Thorstein Veblen, *Theory of the Leisure Class* (New York: Penguin Classics, 1994), 109.

61 *"With the exception of the instinct for self-preservation*　　Ibid., 110, 74.

63 *"Each class envies and emulates*　　Ibid., 103.

63 *"The leisure class . . . stands at the head*　　Ibid., 84.

64 *"As increased industrial efficiency*　　Ibid., 111.

65 *"To the individual of high breeding* Ibid., 187.

66 *For Alain Minc, it's the totality* Alain Minc, *Le Crépuscule des petits dieux* (Paris: Grasset, 2005), 99.

66 *"ordinary citizens of rich countries* Jean Peyrelevade, *Le Capitalisme total* (Paris: Éditions du Seuil, 2005), 53.

68 *the level of English workers' satisfaction* A. E. Clark and A. Oswald, "Satisfaction and Comparison Income," *Journal of Public Economics* 61, no. 3: 359, quoted by Samuel Bowles and Yongjin Park, "Emulation, Inequality, and Work Hours: Was Thorsten Veblen Right?" *The Economic Journal*, November 2005.

68 *And that households with a lower income* J. Schor, *The Overspent American: Upscaling, Downshifting, and the New Consumer* (New York: Basic Books, 1998), quoted by Bowles and Park, "Emulation, Inequality, and Work Hours."

68 *In November 2005,* Ibid.

70 *According to economist Thomas Piketty* Piketty, *L'Économie des inégalités*, 19.

70 *even in China, where, in spite of* Juan Somavia, "430 millions de gens en plus sur le marché du travail dans les dix ans," statements from an interview by Jean-Pierre Robin, *Le Figaro*, 20 June 2006.

70 *"Market theory* Ibid.

71 *"Environmental degradation* OECD, *Environmental Perspectives* (OECD, 2001).

CHAPTER 5

75 *the B61-11* Hervé Kempf, "'Mininuke,' la bombe secrète," *Le Monde*, 21 November 2001.

76 *The kind of oppression that threatens democratic peoples* Alexis de Tocqueville, *Democracy in America*, vol. 2, part 4, chapter 6.

77 *Echelon system* Philippe Rivière, "Le système Échelon," *Le Monde diplomatique*, July 1999.

77 *all, moreover, men and women involved* Christophe Grauwin, *La Croisade des camelots* (Paris: Fayard, 2004).

77 *the Patriot Act* Ibid., 30ff.

78 *It took almost five years for the press to discover* Corine Lesnes, "M. Bush défend la légalité des mesures de surveillance," *Le Monde*, 13 May 2006.

78 *At the same time, people learned that the NSA*   Philippe Gélie, "'Big Brother' espionne les citoyens américains," *Le Figaro*, 13 May 2006.

78 *The NSA, which is part of the Defense Department*   Éric Leser, "National security agency: les oreilles de l'Amérique," *Le Monde*, 1 June 2006.

78 *First intended to be temporary*   Eric Lichtblau and James Risen, "Bank Data Is Sifted by U.S. in Secret to Block Terror," *New York Times*, 23 June 2006.

78 *a piece of legislation adopted in 2001*   Jacques Henno, *Tous fichés* (Paris: Télémaque, 2005), 152.

78 *With respect to the European Union*   Rafaële Rivais, "Fichiers passagers: le Parlement européen peut être contourné," *Le Monde*, 1 June 2006.

79 *In any case, the system*   Corine Lesnes, "La liste des 'interdits de vol' par les autorités américaines comprend au moins trente mille noms," *Le Monde*, 19 May 2006.

79 *author of a book about Bush advisor*   James Moore, *Bush's Brain* (Hoboken, NJ: Wiley, 2003).

79 *Harry Harris opined at the time that the suicides*   Quoted in Corine Lesnes, "Trois suicides à Guantánamo: Bush ne cède pas," *Le Monde*, 13 June 2006.

79 *his top legal advisor Alberto Gonzales*   Alberto Gonzales, memorandum for the President, *Decision Re Application of the Geneva Convention on prisoners of war to the conflict with Al Qaeda and the Taliban*, 25 January 2002, published in *Newsweek*, 24 May 2004.

80 *summarized Larry Cox*   Alan Cowell, "Rights Group Assails 'War Outsourcing,'" *International Herald Tribune*, 24 May 2005.

80 *'enhanced interrogation technique'*   Dick Marty, *Allégations de detentions secrètes et de transferts interétatiques illégaux de détenus concernant des États membres du Conseil de l'Europe*, Conseil de l'Europe (June 2006), 2.

80 *In 2006, close to 14,500 'suspects'*   Sara Daniel, "Tortionnaires sans frontières," *Le Nouvel Observateur*, 12 January 2006.

80 *Several European countries assisted*   Marty, *Allégations de detentions*.

80 *Secretary of State Condoleezza Rice*   Quoted in Corine Lesnes, "Washington stigmatise les abus et les violences pratiqués par plusieurs pays arabes, dont l'Irak," *Le Monde*, 10 March 2006.

80 *In February 2006, Russia adopted*   Marie Jego, "La Russie se dote d'une nouvelle loi antiterroriste," *Le Monde*, 28 February 2006.

80 *In Germany, the* Länder "Trawling for Data Illegal, German Court Rules," *International Herald Tribune*, 24 May 2006.

81 *In Great Britain at the beginning of 2006* Jean-Pierre Langellier, "Londres accusé de violation des droits de l'homme," *Le Monde*, 24 February 2006.

81 *Shortly before, Prime Minister Blair* Rafaële Rivais and Jean-Pierre Stroobants, "Inquiétude croissante en Europe sur la remise en cause de l'État de droit," *Le Monde,* 23 December 2005.

81 *Belgium introduced* Ibid.

81 *In France, in December 2005* Syndicat de la magistrature, "Observations sur le projet de loi n° 2615," November 2005; Patrick Roger, "La France durcit pour la huitième fois en dix ans son arsenal antiterroriste," *Le Monde*, 23 December 2005.

81 *"We are a nation at war* National Security Strategy, March 2006, www.whitehouse.gov/nsc/nss/2006 /.

82 *Type the word 'terrorism', for example* Online consultation, 31 August 2006. On July 1, the scores were 223 million for "terrorism" and 219 million for "democracy."

82 *As the scholar Medhi Belhaj Kacem* Mehdi Belhaj Kacem, *La Psychose française* (Paris: Gallimard, 2006), 40.

82 *In the United States, the number of prisoners* "Mille détenus de plus par semaine aux États-Unis entre mi-2004 et mi-2005," *Le Devoir*, 23 May 2006.

83 *Congress had to establish a commission* Human Rights Watch, *World Report 2006,* 18 January 2006.

83 *Moreover, the quality of "medical and psychiatric care* Ibid.

83 *according to the statistics of the U.S. Bureau of Justice* "Mille détenus," *Le Devoir*.

83 *In France, the incarceration rate* *Le Monde*, 17 February 2006.

83 *The number of prisoners went from* Ministère de la Justice, *Annuaire statistique de la Justice, édition 2006*, La Documentation Française.

83 *the reduction that began in 1996* Geneviève Guérin, "La population carcérale," *ADSP*, no. 44 (September 2003).

83 *That's less than in Germany* International Centre for Prison Studies, www.prisonstudies.org, consulted August 2006.

83 *French laws that increasingly restrict* "Les lois sécuritaires Sarkozy-Perben," Section de Toulon de la Ligue des droits de l'homme, 14 June 2004.

84 *The texts broaden the grounds* "The Principal Measures of the Proposed Law to Prevent Delinquency," *Le Monde*, 28 June 2006; Gilles Sainati, "Justice 2006: petites cuisines et dépendance," May 2006.

84 *the government refused to hold departmental referenda* Hervé Kempf, "Déchets nucléaires: les populations réclament un référendum local," *Le Monde*, 14 September 2005.

84 *the 2003 law requires 10 percent* Law passed 1 August 2003 with respect to local referendum.

85 *hid from the deputies debating the matter* Hervé Kempf, "Le gouvernement a caché des informations aux députés," *Le Monde*, 22 October 2004.

85 *In January 2006, for example* "Trois faucheurs volontaires placés en garde à vue pendant quelques heures," *Le Monde*, 13 January 2006.

86 *Such an unfortunate accident* Armelle Thoraval, "Londres: le fichier ADN grossit, l'inquiétude aussi," *Libération*, 17 January 2006.

86 *four million such cameras in 2004* Clive Norris et al., "The Growth of CCTV," *Surveillance & Society* 2, no. 2-3: 110–35. See www.surveillance-and-society.org.

86 *Police officials are ecstatic* Steve Connor, "You Are Being Watched," *The Independent*, 22 December 2005.

86 *a British Interior Ministry research service* Ibid.

86 *Private inventors create* Yves Eudes, "'Mosquito,' l'arme de dissuasion repousse-ados," *Le Monde*, 15 June 2006.

87 *These transponders have the information capacity* Michel Aberganti, "Mille milliards de mouchards," *Le Monde*, 2 June 2006.

87 *The association Pièces et main-d'oeuvre* Pièces et main-d'oeuvre, "RFID: la police totale," 7 March 2006, pmo.erreur404.org /RFID-la_police_totale.pdf.

88 *George Monbiot envisions* George Monbiot, "Chipping Away at Our Freedom," *The Guardian*, 28 February 2006.

88 *clients of the Baja Beach Club* Yves Eudes, "Digital boys," *Le Monde*, 11 April 2006.

88 *two employees of the Citywatcher Company* Monbiot, "Chipping Away."

88   *In the United States, the director of Verychip*   On *Fox News*, 16 May 2006. Transcribed and cited at the Internet site www.spychips.com.

89   *Some prisoners will soon be equipped*   Emmanuelle Réju, "Le premier bracelet électronique mobile va être expérimenté," *La Croix*, 23 May 2006.

89   *When the children leave the permitted area*   Matt Richtel, "Marketing Surveillance to Parents Who Worry," *New York Times*, reprinted in, *Le Monde*, 13 May 2005.

90   *was it not a so-called liberal weekly*   Jonathan Alter, "Time to Think about Torture," *Newsweek*, 5 November 2001.

90   *"I believe the press was muzzled*   "Irak: une journaliste vedette de CNN critique les médias américains," Agence France Presse, 16 September 2003.

90   *It twice . . . placed long 'investigative' stories*   Michael Gordon and Judith Miller, "U.S. Says Hussein Intensifies Quest for A-bomb Parts," *New York Times*, 8 September 2002; Judith Miller, "After Effects: Prohibited Weapons; Illicit Arms Kept till Eve of War, an Iraqi Scientist Is Said to Assert," *New York Times*, 21 April 2003.

91   *A study of 1,600 television news*   Steve Rendall and Tara Broughel, "Amplifying Officials, Squelching Dissent," FAIR, www.fair.org, May 2003.

92   *"All the press barons*   Servat, "François Pinault, L'invitation au palais."

92   *In Hong Kong, for example*   Sébastien Le Belzic, "Falungong fait de la résistance," *Le Monde 2*, 15 April 2006.

94   *from the pen of sociology professor*   Gunnar Heinsohn, "Babies Win Wars," *Wall Street Journal*, 6 March 2006.

94   *"Using objects leads only to their slow loss*   Jean Baudrillard, *The Consumer Society: Myths and Structure* (London: Sage Publications, 1970).

94   *"It will be necessary to take measures*   Hans Jonas, *The Imperative of Responsibility* (Chicago: University of Chicago Press, 1984).

EPILOGUE

101   *Guattari*   Félix Guattari, *Les Trois Écologies* (Paris: Galilée, 1989), 71.

101   *Dupuy*   Jean-Pierre Dupuy, *Pour un catastrophisme éclairé* (Paris: Éditions du Seuil, 2002), 13.

101   *Barbault*   Robert Barbault, *Un éléphant dans un jeu de quilles* (Paris: Éditions du Seuil, 2006), 186.

102 *Annan*   "Kofi Annan Asserts That Desertification and Drought Constitute Serious Threats to Development," UN News Center, 17 June 2002.

102 *Hama Amadou*   From a speech during the Global Food Summit in Rome, June 2002, FAO.

102 *Brown*   Lester Brown, *Wartime Mobilization to Save the Environment and Civilization,* news release, Earth Policy Institute, 18 April 2006.

102 *Tubiana*   Laurence Tubiana, Worldwatch Institute, *L'État 2006 de la planète* (Geneva: Association L'état de la planète publications, 2006), xii–xiii.

103 *Hirsch*   Martin Hirsch, quoted in Gilles Anquetil and François Armanet, "Comment repenser les inégalités," *Le Nouvel Observateur*, 22 June 2006.

103 *Somavia*   Juan Somavia, "430 millions de gens en plus sur le marché du travail dans les dix ans," statements gathered by Jean- Pierre Robin, *Le Figaro*, 20 June 2006.

103 *Committee for the Abolition*   Committee for the Abolition of Third World Debt, press release, 10 March 2006.

103 *FAO agronomist*   FAO, "Investir dans le secteur agricole pour endiguer l'exode rural," press release, 2 June 2006.

103 *UNDP Expert*   UNDP, *Human Development Report 2005 (*http://hdr .undp.org/en/reports/global/hdr2005/).

104 *Newman*   Robert Newman, "It's Capitalism or a Habitable Planet —You Can't Have Both," *Independent*, 2 February 2006.

104 *Moore*   Michael Moore, *Dude, Where's My Country?* (New York: Warner Books, 2003), 154.

104 *Azam*   Quoted in Alain Caillé, ed., *Quelle démocratie voulons-nous?* (Paris: Editions La Découverte, 2006), 108.

104 *Matouk*   Jean Matouk, "Créer de nouveaux emplois avec une faible croissance," unpublished article, March 2006.

105 *Miller*   Henry Miller, *The Air-Conditioned Nightmare,* (New York: New Directions, 1945), 17.

Also available from Green Books:

FREE TO BE HUMAN

Intellectual self-defence in an age of illusions
David Edwards

*"A wise and acute analysis of the way our minds
are controlled"* – Howard Zinn

While in the West few individuals today suffer
physical restraint by the state, we are still
constrained by powerful psychological chains
– which are in many ways far more effective, if
only because they are so difficult to perceive. *Free to be Human* shows how
we can challenge the 'necessary illusions' of a system that subordinates
people and planet to the drive for profit.

Green Books ISBN 978 1 870098 88 5 288pp £10.95 pb

For our complete booklist, see www.greenbooks.co.uk